# K-Cultuι

*100 Terms to Get You Started with
Korean Popular Culture*

Jikim Publishing

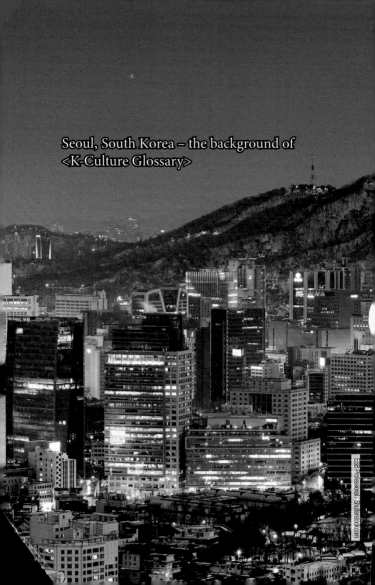

Seoul, South Korea – the background of
<K-Culture Glossary>

K-Culture is a short-historied term referring to South Korean popular culture including various elements – from music, to films, dramas, and fashion, food, comics, and novels.

First published by Jikim Publishing Limited 2021

**Authors** Ji-hyeon Kim, Junyoung Yu, Kathia Sya and Su-hui Son
**Editor** Ji-hyeon Kim, Junyoung Yu and Henry Little
**Book cover design** Hanseoung Pak

If you have any comments or inquiries about this book, please let us
know by email below. Defective products can be exchanged.

**Email** jikimpublishing@gmail.com
**Homepage** www.jikimpublishing.com

**ISBN** 978-1-8380192-2-8 (pbk)
**ISBN** 978-1-8380192-3-5 (ebk)

# K-Culture Glossary

## /케이컬처 글로서리/

*Written by*
Ji-hyeon Kim
Junyoung Yu
Kathia Sya
Su-hui Son

100 Terms to Get You Started with
Korean Popular Culture

# Authors' Preface

K-Culture is a short-historied term referring to South Korean popular culture. The term was first coined in the late 1990s,[1] when various elements of Korean pop culture – from music, to films, dramas, and fashion, food, comics and novels – began to spread overseas, first into neighbouring Asian countries, then further afield. The feverish fondness that Korean pop culture attracted in overseas media soon gave rise to a host of terms such terms as the "Korean Wave" (a.k.a. *Hallyu*), K-Culture, and so on. In fact, the term K-Culture was quickly reimported back into South Korea, where it has been used readily to describe South Korean pop culture.

What is the secret to the ongoing popularity of K-Culture, though? Part of the reason for its success may be found in relation to the institutional, financial and policy support the South Korean government has provided for the movement, continuously and relentlessly working to keep the Korean Wave going and stopping it from becoming a transient phenomenon, all in the hope of enhancing the nation's soft power.[2] Although the political leadership of the country has seen several changes, from Liberal to Conservative, and back to Liberal again, support for K-Culture has remained constant. The government has also expanded and diversified its support into digital domains as the country's cutting-edge IT companies have grown, seeking to foster stronger industrial digital content clusters, thereby propelling the production and consumption of cultural content online, beyond South Korea's national boundaries.

Despite these efforts, it actually took several dec-

-ades for K-Culture to become truly widespread, reaching beyond East and Southeast Asia[3] (areas which share a similar cultural background, with cultural exchanges and Asian pop culture media including Japanese songs and Hong Kong cinema ongoing around the region). Overall, South Korea is still relatively a small country, with a population of 51 million, occupying only the half the Korean peninsula, and still remaining in a state of Cold War with its neighbour to the North. Moreover, its main language, Korean, is used exclusively by Koreans, meaning that attempts to expand its cultural influence in the international markets have often been circumscribed by language barriers. At the same time, and even though digital technologies may have made cultural consumption and sharing on a global level more straightforward, cultural competition against other non-English countries remains fierce.

So what is the historical and cultural context in which K-Culture began to be consumed more widely? Psy's <Gangnam Style>, a worldwide hit in 2012, is widely regarded a tipping point for K-Culture in the global marketplace. While it may be true that this song had a huge influence, however, and despite the language barriers, several Korean TV dramas, films and pop songs had already been gaining a strong reputation within the Asia region prior to this time, thanks in part to the extensive efforts of diverse Korean talent. This book will therefore seek to touch upon other examples that helped to drive the evolution of K-Culture and its spread to a wider audience, even before the emergence of the so-called "K-Pop" phenomenon.

Meanwhile, these days we can see a large fraction

of contemporary K-Culture is indebted to rising public participation in new digital culture genres, for example *Mukbang* and *Webtoons*. These are genres unique to Korean Web culture, and managed to become successful, or even viable, not just thanks to the creative ideas or initiatives of pioneering individuals, but also because the public as a whole was interested in participating in such digitally-driven production formats. Moreover, a significant proportion of K-Culture content today is available free-of-charge, contributing to its easy dissemination across the Internet.

With these pointers in mind, this K-Culture Glossary is designed above all to provide background to this important cultural movement, together with a more detailed analysis of the surrounding trends and phenomena. Of course, living in a Wikipedia era, information regarding most of these glossary terms can be found at the click of a button. Still, we the authors are concerned about the limitations of such information. The four authors who have participated in this glossary are either professionals in the Korean cultural industry or researchers of Korean culture, and we have found a large proportion of information on the Web to contain distorted facts, misleading information, inaccurate data, poor translations and superficial explanations. Thus, we have taken the initiative to compile this glossary, making use of our combined expertise and cultural knowledge. Covering 100 key terms – those we find most important for understanding K-Culture today – through a series of discussions, fact-checks, and peer reviews, we hope to elaborate on their meaning via detailed explanations and expert commentary.

At the same time, all of us agreed that such a glossary should be written in an easily digestible and concise form, and that it should be fun to read for anyone who likes or is interested in K-Culture. Generally, the beginning and development of fandom for any culture starts with a community coming together, a process whereby people come to share their interests and tastes, and exchange emotions and form new friendships, joined together by their shared interest.

Happily most of the authors of this glossary are based in East London, a place where one can find hipsters relishing *Kimchi* cheese toasties while listening to BTS and Blackpink songs. One of the authors, while attending her COVID-19 vaccination appointment, even met a doctor and nurse who enjoyed watching Korean dramas on Netflix and who tried to calm her down in Korean! If this book could help make such aficionados and friends of K-Culture a little happier, and if they could share their happiness with their friends and connections (and with us, too!), we can think of no greater satisfaction for our work. There would be no greater pleasure on earth.

# Authors' Biography

## Ji-hyeon Kim / Media researcher

Ji-hyeon earned a doctorate in Cultural Studies from Goldsmiths, University of London, and has since been teaching media theory and popular culture at several UK universities. Her research concentrates on South Korean popular culture and digital media. She has developed her interest in independent publishing through her research on self-publishing as mnemotechnics. In conjunction with this, in 2020 she established Jikim Publishing Limited – the first enterprise in the UK that publishes a series of guidebooks of South Korean Culture. <K-Culture Glossary> is the second book of the series.

## Junyoung Yu / Media researcher

Junyoung is a Visiting Fellow in Media and Communications at the London School of Economics and Political Science. As a sociologist of media, his research is concerned primarily with the intersection of data technologies, digital platforms, algorithmic systems and social life, and how the newly emergent socio-material environment of communication shapes the way we live everyday life. His interest has also recently extended into digital platforms in South Korea (such as Kakao and Naver), and relatedly he authored an article on the shifting cultural production and digital labour in the Korean platform contexts.

**Kathia Sya  / Founder of personal care brand**

Kathia's formative experience in the world of skincare began in 1987, when she accompanied her mother, a Paris-trained aesthetician, starting a spa business in the northern states of Malaysia. Her interest in cosmetics has since deepened, taking her through the highs and lows of each emerging industry, from J-Beauty, T-Beauty and since 2005, K-Beauty. She has since served as the first Beauty Editor for <Tongue In Chic>, Southeast Asia's top fashion lifestyle web magazine. She holds an MA in Sociology from Goldsmiths, University of London. She is also trained as a perfumer and founded her personal care brand: Drops of Humanity in 2015.

**Su-hui Son / TV producer**

Su-hui is an expert in Korean broadcasting, film and feminism, currently working in the South Korean public broadcasting service. Over the past 10 years, she has produced a broad range of entertainment shows, such as <Singing Battle> and <Hello Counsellor> at the KBS (Korean Broadcasting System). Presently, she is interested in directing and presenting women's stories to the world. In this book, she identifies some of the recent trends regarding South Korean films and feminism. She holds a BA in Media Studies and an MA in Cultural Studies, both from Hankuk University of Foreign Studies, South Korea.

# 1.
## Aegyo
### /애교/

An attitude of cuteness towards others; a display of affection via cuteness of voice, facial expressions and coquettish gestures. In the past, *aegyo* was a term mainly used by women and children, and as such, was considered a gendered language resource that helped women form their identity.[4]

In recent years, however, as gender roles have become less fixed in South Korean society, the term *aegyo* has become more widely used by young people, in a broader range of settings and regardless of gender. Idol singers, for example, often show *aegyo* to their fans on stage or at fan-sign events. As the "Korean Wave" (a.k.a. *Hallyu*) spreads across the world, moreover, *aegyo* is a term increasingly used by fans overseas.

# 2.
## Aegyosal
## /애교살/

While *aegyo* typically refers to baby-cuteness, or more accurately a form of youthful winsomeness, and is a term used widely across many areas of popular culture, in K-Beauty, the most commonly used phrase containing the word *aegyo* is *aegyosal*.

    *Aegyosal* refers to the little pockets of fat that protrude below the eyes whilst smiling. This feature is most prominent on babies, and the *aegyosal* sits directly below the lower eye lid. It is not to be mistaken for the bags under the eyes that occur in older people, which are to be found further from the lower lid, due to weakened muscles.[5]

    *Aegyosal*-inspired makeup trends first emerged in 2013.[6] Makeup looks based around the *aegyosal* concept accentuate the fat pouches under the eyes when smiling, yielding a perceived youthfulness.[7]

# 3.
# Afreeca TV
# /아프리카 TV/

*Afreeca TV* is the short name for "A(ny) Free (TV broad) ca(sting)".[8] Based in South Korea, it provides "real-time" (live) video sharing as its main service. A beta service was launched in 2005, with official trading commencing in March 2006. *Afreeca TV* offers an average of 100,000 streaming broadcasts daily, drawing a combined viewership of up to 360,000 and gaining audience numbers as much as three times the size of rival Korean cable channels by 2013.[9] Th number of subscribers reached 6.86 million by September 2016, contributing to a steady increase in sales from 2011 onwards.[10]

It is important to note that South Korean society provided a special environment for the growth of *Afreeca TV*. Korea is an "IT power" and as such has experienced rapid expansion of broadband services and smart devices, making it possible for the rapid proliferation of production and consumption of UCC in Korean society. Even before the emergence of live video services, South Korea had become an "online gaming empire",[11] with an enthusiastic sub-culture highly receptive to special broadcasting contents and game broadcasting forming around novel cable broadcasting companies.

Thus, it was no coincidence that, when it first started, the *Afreeca TV* platform was called "*Afreeca Game TV*", clearly indicating the need for broadcasting reflecting the interactivity of online games among young Korean people.[12] The inflow of users brought about both quantitative and qualitative expansions of content, as well as an increase in the number of viewers. Consequently, as *Afreeca TV* changed its name from "Game TV" into "*Afreeca*" (Any Free TV broadcasting), it matured as a mass media platform streaming live videos on diverse topics such as food and cooking. In 2009, for example, videos tagged "*Mukbang*" started to appear on *Afreeca TV*. Showing a broadcaster eating a lot of food, they went viral around the world in the years that followed.[13]

# 4.
## Aggro
### /어그로/

An Internet neologism derived from "aggro", English slang for rude or aggressive behaviour. It was first used as a term in eSports referring to techniques that provoke opponents' reactions,[14] but gradually began to be used in other areas of South Korean pop culture. For example, the expression "attracting aggro" is often used to refer to the activities that create a dispute among users, for example posting of articles that do not fit with a topic to attract the attention of others, or posting of articles on controversial topics. Individuals who seek to attract aggro are sometimes labelled "*guan-sim-jongja*" (관심종자).

# 5.
## Akpul
## /악플/

Abbreviation for malicious comments or exchanges. Those who leave malicious comments are called "*akpul-leo*". This is regarded as a chronic disease in South Korean Internet culture. *Akpul* on news items about celebrities, athletes, politicians and other well-known figures has become so severe that one of the largest web portals, Daum (owned by Kakao), temporarily removed the comments sections in its Entertainment News.[15]

      *Akpul* is also considered a serious concern in the *Webtoon* industry, which has become one of the major growth engines for the country. Fundamentally working on freelance contracts, with relatively little legal protection, it is something most *Webtoonists* (*Webtoon* creators) find difficult to deal with.[16]

# 6.
## Altang
## /알탕/

Originally, *altang* referred to "*tang*", a class of soup-like dishes in Korean cuisine using pollock roe. However, recently in the Korean cultural scene, it has been used to negatively characterise films where all the major roles are played by male actors.[17] For instance, many Korean gangster films are often referred to as "*altang movies*", as female characters in such films often assume only passive or supporting roles.

## The current address of
## women in film in Korea?

Try to think of a female character in Korean cinema taking a lead role or taking the initiative. Do any memorable female characters spring to mind? Sadly, this is not the case. This is inevitable, given that prior to the COVID-19 pandemic, all the leading Korean films, those that mobilised audiences of 10 million or more, were directed by male directors, featuring male characters in the lead role.[18]

On the other hand, in 2018, 59% of those admitted to departments of theatre, drama or film for study at Korean universities were women, even despite which the percentage of female directors in the same year was only around 10%.[19] What could this mean? Among the films released in the last decade, from 2009 to 2018, the number of films from female directors actually decreased, from 13.2% to 12.3%, 1% down from 10 years before.[20]

Where have all the female filmmakers gone?

Fortunately, in the independent film scene today, female filmmakers are fairly prominent. A prime example is director Kim Bo-ra, whose <House of Hummingbird > (2019), was praised as the <Parasite> (2019) of the independent film world. Produced with a budget of 300 million KRW (approximately US $270,000), <House of Hummingbird> swept 60 domestic and international film festivals (it may be close to winning another award now) and mobilised

147,461 viewers. In particular, <House of Hummingbird> was praised by Alison Bechdel, inventor of the Bechdel Test, for its heroic story, featuring a teenage girl at the forefront of the action.[21]

Speaking of the Bechdel test, last year a "2020 Bechdel Day" symposium was held, with the aim of promoting gender-equal Korean films, prompting what seems to be an encouraging process of change. Overall, the symposium sought to introduce "films that feature at least two women" who took the initiative to talk about subjects without hatred, discrimination, or stereotypes, and in 2020, it selected 10 films: <Kim Ji-young, Born 1982> (2019), <Maggie> (2018), <Another Child> (2019), <House of Hummingbird> (2018), <Our Body> (2018), <Baseball Girl> (2019), <The House of Us> (2019), <Moonlit Winter> (2019), <Lucky Chan-sil> (2019) and <A French Woman> (2019).[22]

To introduce two of these in this limited space: set in 1994 in Daechi-dong, Seoul, <House of Hummingbird> depicts plainly the experiences of Eun-hee, a middle school girl who suffers from the absurdity and violence of the patriarchal system.

<Lucky Chan-sil>, meanwhile, is the debut feature of Kim Cho-hee, a former producer who used to work for world-renowned Korean "*auteur*" director Hong Sang-soo. Chan-sil had spent her entire life in filmmaking, but became unemployed after the director she was working with suddenly died. Thus, she started to worry about how she would make a living, and based on her lived experience,

the film provides audiences with messages of hope and consolation.

# 7.
## Ampoule
### /앰플/

The modern ampoule refers to a kind of packaging format involving a hermetically sealed vial of glass. It was invented in the 1890's by French pharmacist Stanislas Limousin to store and transport pharmacological liquids in a sterile state.[23] Eventually, the cosmetics industry began to adopt the use glass ampoules to preserve concentrated actives. This format helps prevent oxidation and spoilage of skincare formulas with a high concentration of actives.

The content of skincare ampoules are usually simplified formulas designed for single-use. Ampoule contents differ from serums in being formulated with multiple functions. The glass ampoule remains popular with French pharmacy hair and skincare brands for delivering treatments for domestic use. Users need to snap the neck of the glass vial in order to access the contents. This also makes it a tamper-proof mode of packaging. However, there is a risk of broken glass, should users accidentally drop one.

When K-Beauty producers revived the popularity of the ampoule they did not revive the glass vial packaging, but they revived the spirit of the concept, making it a short-hand for cosmetic concentrates. The K-Beauty ampoule is similar to its French counterpart in that it focuses on delivering a concentrated dose of active ingredients. These actives are also found in comparably higher concentrations than in serums. However, unlike the French vials, the K-Beauty ampoule also does away with the hassle of hermetically sealed glass, instead using other, more modern packaging and formula stabilising methods. To add to the confusion, some brands who have made their name creating accessible ampoule ranges are now returning to the glass vial format to visually and functionally distinguish ampoules from serums in different retail environments.[24]

Popular ingredients marketed in ampoules today include Vitamin C, Propolis and anti-pigmentation actives. They are sometimes used interchangeably with the term serum, so it is important to read the label to see if you are getting a multi-benefit formula or a focused formula delivering a single-active ingredient.

When K-Beauty producers revived the popularity of the ampoule they did not revive the glass vial packaging, but they revived the spirit of the concept, making it a shorthand for cosmetic concentrates.

*

## The difference between
## ampoules and serums

Another product category with roots in continental European skincare. Often used interchangeably with the term ampoule by bloggers or media. However, within K-beauty, the distinction between ampoules and serum is still observed in the formulas. Serums tend to be multi-function formulas with a focus on delivering a synergistic boost of functions within a daily skincare routine. It slots in typically after a hydrator or a toner, but before a moisturiser.

Serums can contain multiple active ingredients in a hydrating base. Serums can be formulated to cater to a variety of skincare goals. However, unlike the focus on single active ingredients in ampoules, formulators will include several actives at suitable concentrations in a daily use formula to achieve that goal.[25]

# 8.
# Baedal minjok
## /배달의 민족/

*Baedal minjok*, abbreviated as "*Baemin*", is the name of a South Korean food delivery start-up. *Baedal* was a term used widely in the Japanese colonial period to mark Korean national identity, while *minjok* can loosely be translated as ethnic group.[26] However, since *Baedal* is a homonym, also meaning "delivery", the start-up took it as a double entendre, using the slogan "What kinds of *minjok* are we?", causing confusion for many.

# 9.
## Baewoonim
/배우님/

A compound word comprising "*baewoo*" (actor/actress) and the honorific suffix "*-nim*". It is often used by the fandom to refer to an actor/actress whom they like or respect for their competence.

In Korean grammar, "*-nim*" is not normally attached to nouns, and is used only in limited instances, such as to a few specific words that refer to a social status or position, ultimately denoting respect.

# 10.
# Bangpan
# /방판/

Similar to the "Avon lady" or Mary Kay network of direct salespersons, a culturally significant door-to-door beauty consultant. Amorepacific formed their door-to-door sales network in the 1960s and have kept them running ever since.[27] *Bangpan* consultants remain popular, and companies have exclusive lines only available through their networks. They were also a regular feature of the hit TV series <Reply 1988>. The series formed a historic snapshot of *Bangpan* consultants, and the conviviality that accompanies them.

# 11.
## Base makeup
## /베이스 메이크업/

A term popular in Korean and Japanese colour cosmetic industry to describe skin makeup. This can include products of all types such as foundations, concealers, primers, tinted moisturisers, finishing powders, BB and CC creams.

Base makeup as a product category distinguishes itself from colour makeup, which is referred to as point makeup. The term base makeup is also widely understood in many parts of East Asia and South East Asia, where Korean and Japanese beauty exports dominate.

# 12.
# BB
## /비비/

BB stands for Blemish Balm, now a product category due to its popularity in the early and mid-2000s in South Korea and East and South East Asia. The product that inspired this category was originally developed by a German dermatologist Dr Christine Schrammek for clients who needed a product in their routine to support post-procedure skin (laser or acid peels leave the skin in need of good SPF and redness coverage to unify the look of healing skin, and skin calming active ingredients).[28]

BB cream was initially developed as a single product, and whereas traditional base makeup relied largely on colour pigments for coverage, BB cream offered a simplified formula dependent on reflectors and Titanium Dioxide or Zinc Oxide.[29] This allowed for less extensive application while achieving a high coverage and remain sensitive skin-friendly. However, this presented a colour matching issue, as the high concentrations of reflectors can leave skin looking grey. This dampened the popularity of BB cream as other types of base makeup started to catch up with new, multi-functional formulations.

Even today, BB cream has not left the market as a product category. Recently, it has inspired more base makeup product ranges for men, partly thanks to its ease of use. It is also making a strong return in form of ultra-fine formulas.

This aims to meet "*padepri*" (파데프리; a combination of the words "foundation" and "free"; see entry 87) and "MSBB" (My Skin But Better) trends in the wake of the pandemic.

# 13.
# Bedaet
# /베댓/

As most web portals in South Korea provide news and Web-toons free of charge, they attract a plethora of comments and responses from Internet users. While some of them are controversial for their potential harmfulness in terms of affecting public opinion-formation, others are seen useful for providing up-to-date information and news. In case of *Webtoons*, the accompanying comments serve as a proxy for emotional reactions against the *Webtoon*, and also as the space for a critical community where different views and interpretations can intersect. To prevent malicious comments or advertisement from gaining prominence, Kakao and Naver operate a system that prioritises the comments and responses that receive the largest number likes, follow-up comments, and recommendations.

These popular comments are dubbed "best comments", or *bedaet*. In the case of several popular *Webtoons*, those which attract hundreds and thousands of readership immediately on release, many users comment and compete to make their own comments the "best comment". Some mainstream media note that there is even a trend to best comments first, before the actual *Webtoon*, naming this trend "reply-cation".[30]

# 14.
## Bedo
### /베도/

A Naver-run, (user-created) comic bulletin board on which anyone can participate. It is an online space included in the portal's Webtoon service, where amateur cartoonists compete against one another. Those who receive the highest audience ratings and reactions will get an opportunity to officially publish and serialise their work on the Naver's main Webtoon platform, under their production guidance.[31]

# 15.
# Bibimbap
## /비빔밥/

*Bibimbap*, one of Korea's representative traditional foods, is known for cooking which follows the principles of the five elements and *yin and yang* philosophies. *Yin and yang* define the universe as the interaction of two opposite forces, and the five elements theory separates this dynamic interaction further into five stages of transformation. *Bibimbap* is complete through the process of arranging appropriately *yin and yang* ingredients on the rice and mixing them together harmoniously.

Five different colours of ingredients are used: green (spinach), red (chili paste and carrots), yellow (egg yolk), white (radish and bellflower), and black (shiitake mushrooms, fiddleheads and beef).[32]

# 16.
## Bojagi
## /보자기/

Wrapping things or foods with cloth "*bojagi*" is a unique textile culture in Korea, dating back more than 200 years, all the way to the Joseon Dynasty. *Bojagi* are generally made of *jaturi* (자투리), small pieces of patchwork left over from clothes making or fabric cutting. Historically, completed *bojagi* were mainly used for storing valuable items or foods; sometimes, they were used also as a wrapping paper for precious and expensive gifts. For example, wrapping wedding gifts in *bojagi* was considered a ritual that could bring luck, since etymologically *bojagi* also meant wrapping "*bok*" (복; meaning happiness and luck). So *bojagi* were not only used for practical reasons, they were also given symbolic value, as treasure troves of people's devotions and aspirations.[33] Through the process of painstakingly seaming *jaturis* to make *bojagi*, many become beautiful ornaments in themselves, so becoming a form of cultural heritage, giving them an opportunity to be re-evaluated as a kind of art.

In fact, recently *bojagi* have received serious recognition both domestically and internationally, as a cultural heritage unique to Korea. In particular, the styling is used in different ways in the Anglo-American fashion world. The French luxury brand Hermès, for example, in 2019 launched a series of scarves entitled the *"Art of Bojagi"* (*L'Art du Bojagi*), with the brand's artistic director Pierre-Alexis Dumas

drawing inspiration from traditional Korean culture.[34] Meanwhile, textile artist Adam Pogue displayed several quilt works in 2019 that were inspired by *bojagi*.[35]

# 17.
## Bromance
## /브로맨스/

A compound word of "brother" and "romance", referring to the intimate and deep friendship between men. The term has gained prominence since 2013 in the Korean cultural industry when <Shinsegae>,[36] a film about a friendship between a gangster and an undercover police officer, attracted 4 million viewers. It has since been used frequently in film and drama marketing. For example, a promotional article for an ongoing Netflix drama <Navilera> (2021) depicts the relationship between two protagonists – Deok-chul (Park In-hwan) who started ballet at the age of 70, and Chae-rok (Song Kang), a 23-year-old ballerino feeling lost facing the reality, as a "ballet bromance".[37] The term is sometimes confused with boy love (BL), which refers to love between men, but unlike BL, bromance does not connote any physical or sexual relation.

# 18.
# BTS
## /방탄소년단/

BTS is arguably "the biggest boy band" in the current K-Pop scene. It is an acronym for the official name *Bangtan Sonyeondan* (Bulletproof Boys). With the word "*bangtan*" literally meaning bulletproof in Korean, the band's name shows their desire to resist the impact of bullet-like prejudice towards teenagers and younger generations.[38]

Debuting in 2013 with the <2 COOL 4 SKOOL> album, they swept the awards season that year, winning several Best New Artist awards. 5 years on, they started entering Anglo-American music charts with the album <LOVE YOURSELF 轉 "Tear">. This and the follow-up album <LOVE YOURSELF 結 "Answer"> became the first album from a Korean band to debut at number one on the US Billboard 200, attracting global attention. The album <MAP OF THE SOUL : PERSONA> released in 2019 also reached number one on the Billboard 200.

With the worldwide outbreak of COVID-19 in early 2020, most K-Pop bands cancelled their plan to tour around the world, so sales in overseas markets were expected to stagnate. However, in August 2020, BTS released a new digital single <Dynamite>, which topped the Billboard Hot 100 for three weeks running. This upbeat disco-pop about finding joy for the little things in life reflected the band's desire to "energise and deliver happiness" to those suffering

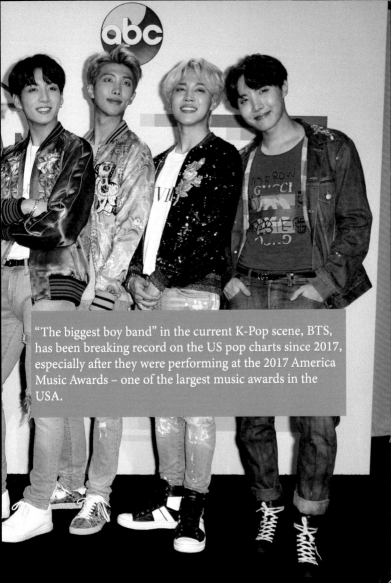

"The biggest boy band" in the current K-Pop scene, BTS, has been breaking record on the US pop charts since 2017, especially after they were performing at the 2017 America Music Awards – one of the largest music awards in the USA.

from the prolonged COVID-19 crisis.[39]

Including important social messages in their albums is a distinguishing feature of BTS's music. As mentioned in Jikim Publishing's first publication <Bumping into BTS>, their previous albums were intended to send comfort to teenagers and young adults troubled by their identity, telling them to love themselves, while being frequently critical of older customs and generations. This was why the US magazine <Rolling Stone> noted how BTS were "breaking K-Pop's biggest taboos" by speaking openly about taboo subjects in South Korea, like LGBT+, adolescent mental health issues and social pressure to succeed, raising public awareness while maintaining a respectable self-image, thereby helping to lessen people's dislike about the K-Pop engine as a whole.[40]

BTS is also known for its participation in various campaigns for social change. From 2016 they have been participating in the UNICEF "ENDviolence" campaign aimed at protecting children and teenagers from violence, with individual members making several generous donations to the cause. BTS's official fandom, ARMY ("Adorable Representative M.C. for Youth"), also often participate in such charitable activities, helping to make an even greater splash.[41]

# 19.
# Bunsik
# /분식/

*Bunsik* originally referred to flour-based foods, such as *Janchi-guksu* (banquet noodles). However, over time its meaning has been extended to encompass street foods, including flour-based snacks like *tteokbokki* (stir-fried rice cakes) and *twigim* (tempura-like snacks), as well as non-flour-based ones such as *gimbap* (rice roll made of a sheet of dried seaweed) and *soondae* (Korean black pudding). For example, "*Bunsik-jib*" is a mash-up of *bunsik* and *jib* which means house, and it now refers to a small bistro or kiosk that sells various kinds of aforesaid snacks and street foods such as noodles, dumplings, *tteokbokki*, and *gimbap*. Related to this, a noteworthy word is "*gim-tteok-soon*", a neologism of the first syllables of three arguably most representative and popular street foods in Korea – *gimbap, tteokbokki, and soondae.*

While these are three different dishes, many Korean street bistros and food stalls (*pojang-macha*) sell them together as a set menu, promoting them as "*gim-tteok-soon*", contributing to the widespread use of the term.

One of the most popular tourist attractions in South Korea is to take a walk through the traditional village of Bukchon wearing rented *hanbok*, and have *bunsik* in a snack restaurant.

# 20.
# Byeoljeom
## /별점/

User ratings for Webtoons online. The highest rating is 5 stars, corresponding to 10 points. The star rating averages the ratings given by multiple users, and can be used as a standard against which to select a new Webtoon to read. When a Webtoonist does not meet a deadline or when s/he expresses a specific worldview or political view through their work, many users deliberately give it low star ratings as an appeal. This act of lowering a star rating is called "star rating terrorism".

# 21.
## CC
### /씨씨/

The definition of the initials CC is somewhat contested. Some of the most popular definitions include Colour Correction, Colour Change and Colour Control. The use of the double-lettered initials also help consumers identify it as a product category similar to BB in terms of ease of use. CC products typically claim to feature more cosmetically elegant formulas to BBs, focusing on getting the right combination of redness-diffusing colour pigments in addition to more traditional reflectors to unify skin tone discolouration without heavy reliance on foundations or skin-matching reflective pigments like those found in BBs.

Unlike BBs, CCs were not always formulated with the same focus on SPF or skincare functions. However, over time, the line between the two has become blurred, and dermo-cosmetic functions are increasingly common across both.[42] From our observation of the market, CC remain the first choice when brands choose to feature a larger range of colours.

Much like BB creams, CC also inspired a series of global brands to adapt the concept – from French dermo-cosmetic brands looking for a more cosmetically elegant tint for rosacea patients, to premium brands looking to meet customer demand for elusive products that are easy to apply but that also deliver the "MSBB" (My Skin But Better) finish.

CC products focus on getting the right combination of redness-diffusing colour pigments in addition to more traditional reflectors to unify skin tone discolouration without heavy reliance on foundations.

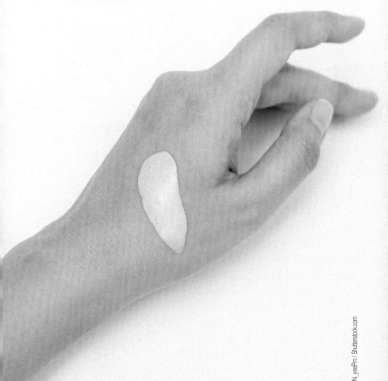

# 22.
# Chaebol
# /재벌/

A mash-up of *chae* (meaning wealth in Korean), and *bol* (meaning clan), *chaebol* was originally derived from the Japanese word *zaibatsu* (財閥), and has been used to refer to syndicate of capitalists tied by family or personal relations. While it is a vocabulary distinctive to South Korea's economic system, it also has many negative connotations. First and foremost, criticism has been raised that the contemporary *chaebol*-dominated structure of the Korean economy has its roots in the crony capitalism that prevailed during the rapid economic growth of the 1970s, and which resulted in the concentration of wealth within a few individuals and families who participated in large-scale government-led projects.[43]

The term *chaebol* is a seminal one in the cultural industry, too, as a staple of the narratives of many Korean TV dramas. A study by Hae-nyeon Lee (2006) revealed that the most popular dramas in Korea, those with an audience rating of more than 40%, tended to feature storylines with a male *chaebol* protagonist falling in love with an ordinary female protagonist with a Cinderella complex.[44] Some scholars suggest this reflects current trends in Korean society where materialism is expanding, with the ideal male portrayed of previous Korean TV dramas shifting away from self-made men like judges, attorneys and politicians towards *chaebol* people born with a silver spoon in their mouths.[45]

On the other hand, it has been argued that interpretations of female characters as having Cinderella complexes are little more than sexist, as women who date *Chaebol* men (as in the popular drama <Boys over Flowers>) are not necessarily financially dependent on their wealth.[46]

# 23.
# Choeae
## /최애/

A K-Pop fandom term and compound of Sino-Korean letters "*choe*" and "*ae*", which mean "the most" and "love". Fans refer to their favourite idol group members as their choeae, and the second favourite as their chaae, a compound of "*cha*" and "*ae*", where the former means "next".

# 24.
# Chokchok
## /촉촉/

Plump with moisture. Texturally likened to a fresh grape full of moisture. Indicative of healthy skin barrier function that is able to retain moisture effectively. *Chokchok* is a key measure of the effectiveness of basic skincare routines. This may be represented as a natural satin glow in makeup looks.

# 25.
# Chonggong
## /총공/

An abbreviation for "*chong-gonggyuk*" (총공격) meaning a full-scale attack using all troops and equipment. In K-Pop fandom, it refers to a fan club of an idol band together giving a full support to them, mobilising all means available. For example, it is used to encourage fan activities that can help promote idol bands, from "streaming rotation" (repeatedly playing the bands' songs to improve their ranking on the music charts); increasing the number of YouTube views and comments; participating in popularity votes through both texts and on the Web; and so on.[47]

# 26.
# Cica
# /시카/

Cica is not a skincare ingredient and is not synonymous with popular skin healing ingredient centella asiatica. A majority but not all products prefixed with cica- contain centella asiatica derivatives. Global and K-Beauty brands have used the term cica to indicate that their products cater to healing and protecting sensitive skin. Cica comes from the term cicatrix, the scientific term for a flat scar that forms following changes or injury to the skin layer.[48]

Cica is now often used by makeup producers to indicate whole product categories. Some of the earliest uses can be traced to French cult dermocosmetic product, Cicaplast, by La Roche Posay.[49] K-Beauty producers retained the dermocosmetic visual identity of their French counterparts when creating their own interpretation of the cica skincare category. The K-Beauty equivalents focused heavily on centella asiatica derivatives unlike their French equivalents. K-Beauty producers also tended to develop the cica skincare concept into full range of daily skincare for sensitive, acne-prone or post-procedure compared to their French counterparts tended to focus on targeted use treatments.

*

## Centella asiatica in Korean?
## Byeongpul (병풀)

Centella asiatica goes by the common name "*byeongpul*" in Korea. It is a popular ingredient with skin healing properties.[50] It is also referred to by its colloquial names, Gotu Kola, Indian Pennywort or Asian Tiger Grass. Despite its recent popularity as a skincare ingredients, centella asiatica has widespread use in cuisine and holistic medicine in South Asian and South East Asian cuisine.[51] The commonly isolated skincare actives from centella asiatica include Asiaticoside, Asiatic Acid, Madecassoside and Madasiatic Acid.

# 27.
# Cleanbot
# /클린봇/

One of the most chronic diseases of Korean web culture is considered *akpul* (malicious comments). Naver, the largest web portal in the country, has developed a new malicious comment detection AI titled "Cleanbot 2.0" on June 18, 2020, with a view to solving the issues with *akpul* and dealing with them.[52]

Cleanbot 2.0 categorises certain expressions that commonly appear in malicious comments, including:

- Swearing: general swear words, included in Naver's swearword database
- Vulgar expressions: rude, disrespectful expressions that are offensive to others
- Obscene expressions: sexually arousing, lewd, or pornographic expressions
- Violent expressions: expressions about physical threats and violence
- Discriminatory expressions: expressions of discrimination based on region, ethnicity, country, religion, etc.
- Derogatory expressions: expressions causing humiliation and shame

Presently, Naver's *Webtoon* service runs Cleanbot to detect such comments, and filter those that may cause problems.

# 28.
# Coin
# /코인/

A term referring to the online credits used to pay for *Webtoons*. Coins are also used for purchasing web novels. Generally these credits are called "coin", but they have different names according to each platform: for Naver it is "cookie". For this reason, charging credits are sometimes called "baking cookies".[53] One cookie is worth 100 KRW (US 10c).

# 29.
# Cushion
## /쿠션/

Cushion formats have become a dominant feature of
K-Beauty colour and base makeup products. This product
delivery format was first used by Amorepacific in 2008 to
launch a cushion compact under their IOPE brand.[54]

Cushions are often spoken of in reference to
foundation or base cosmetics. Since its launch for use with
lightweight BB skin makeup, cushion delivery formats have
been applied to sunscreen, liquid blush, liquid lip colour and
foundations. The cushion format allows for very light and
fluid formulas to be applied efficiently and easily. This means
producers do not need to thicken formulas for spreadability.
Layering thus becomes easier and more foolproof for the
consumer. More importantly, it allows for consumers to
marry the use of liquid products with a convenience usually
associated with powder makeup.

South Korean producers remain the key producers
of cushion format cosmetics, with Amorepacific holding on
to its patent until the cosmetics giant lost its case in 2018.[55]
The cushion format has also become the most coveted
format for international cosmetic brands, and a key area
of competition since its introduction to the global cosmetics market.[56] Since its launch, the cushion format has also
inspired a variety of similar delivery formats, such as tension
mesh and press-to-dispense compacts.

# 30.
# Daetgeul
## /댓글/

A pure Korean word meaning "comment" or "reply" on Internet posts. It was introduced to the common lexicon at the behest of the National Institute of Korean Language as a means of moderating the impact of foreign languages. *Akpul*, by contrast, is an Internet neologism and compound of "*ak*" (meaning evil, wickedness) and "*pul*" (meaning reply), referring specifically to malicious comments or cyber bullying (See entry 5).

# 31.
# Dalgona
# /달고나/

A coffee drink made with instant coffee, sugar, water and milk. It has two distinct layers: (a) whipped coffee cream (made by mixing instant coffee, sugar and hot water in a 1:1:1 ratio and whipping more than 400 times) sitting on top of (b) iced milk. As COVID-19 became widespread in the country, so people stayed at home, many Korean people tried this initially as a way to kill time, but then uploaded their efforts to YouTube, Instagram, and TikTok, as part of social media challenges, making it a popular social media trend.

Similar recipes were already available in other countries, as in "beaten coffee", "Indian cappuccino", or "café batido a mano". However, as the recipe gained a renewed popularity during the pandemic while being spread around Korean social media, it has been re-labelled as a "South Korean coffee treat" (BBC), or more popularly "*dalgona* coffee", named after one of the Korean sweets *dalgona* for their similar taste and flavour.

Making *dalgona* coffee is fairly similar to whisking egg whites into a meringue. Protein in instant coffee crystals trap air and sugar provides stability by absorbing some of the water, helping to create a sticky meringue-like coffee foam. This is why using instant coffee is recommended on YouTube and TikTok videos, as normal ground coffee contains much less protein per gram.

One Korean science magazine even introduced a more science-based recipe that "To speed up the foam-making, dissolve instant coffee in lukewarm water, and then add sugar once the temperature has dropped".[57] See also the recipe on BBC which promises higher success rate when using western ingredients.[58]

---

*

## How to make Dalgona coffee

1. Prepare instant coffee, sugar, water, and milk. Normal ground coffee may not work well in making the foam.

2. Dissolve instant coffee in lukewarm water, and whip quickly with spoon, whisk, or electric hand-held mixer. The ratio of coffee and water should be 1:1.

3. Once the temperature of coffee and water mixture has dropped, add sugar and keep whipping, until it is light brown, fluffy and sticky, holding some stiff peaks when the whisk is removed. It may require around 400 whips.

4. Spoon dollops of the frothed coffee mixture on iced milk (hot if desired), or water. Serve.

# 32.
# Deokhu
## /덕후/

A term originating from the Japanese word "*otaku*" (お た く ), denoting people who consume their interests passionately, especially anime and manga. It has been reformulated as "*deokhu*" to make it sound more Sino-Korean. In Korea, *deokhu* is used to refer to those pursuing a deep interest in any field, rather than anime or manga alone. It began to be used in the mid-2000s,[59] and is now considered everyday language, at least online, so there are many derivatives from this term. For instance, "*deok-jil-hada*" means engaging in *deokhu*-like activities.

  In other cases, some Sino-Korean words are combined to mean various things: becoming a *deokhu* is called "*ipdeok*" (입덕); having a break from *deok-jil* is called "*hudeok*" (휴덕); quitting *deok-jil* is called "*taldeok*" (탈덕).

  Other derivatives include "*seongdeok*" (성덕), which is a short for "*seonggonghan deokhu*" (meaning "a successful deokhu"), and "*deokjil mate*", referring to those who have become friends by being fans of the same idol group.[60]

# 33.
# Deugael
# /드갤/

A term referring to the category of drama-related communities operated within a South Korean Internet forum called "Digital Camera Inside (DCInside)". This is often referred to in the shortened form: "*deugael*". Here, opinions about TV dramas are freely exchanged, for users' privacy is protected by full anonymity. Another prominent feature of *deugael* is the active sharing of forms of information and materials, including the promotional products provided by broadcasters, to user-generated content relating to the dramas. Those working in the Korean broadcasting industry tend to consider the vibrance of these communities as a proxy for the popularity of dramas. In fact, many entertainment-related news often quotes the posts and opinions from the *deugael* as "public reactions".[61]

# 34.
# Donginnyeo
## /동인녀/

The word "*dongin*" means a person who shares similar goals and hobbies. Since the 1980s, several young female consumers have formed a subcultural group, centring on sharing reviews of cultural content (such as cartoons, animations, novels, dramas, and films), about homosexuality, and sometimes creating fan fictions and publishing them as independent magazines and books. Since then, these consumers have been referred to as "*donginnyeo*". Here, "*-nyeo*" is the suffix which refers a woman.

In the mid-2000s, as homosexual cultural content started gaining popularity in mainstream Korean cultural content, there have been claims from both the mass media and academia that donginnyeo should be evaluated seriously for its own sake, as a gender-empowered taste community and cultural production group.[62]

# 35.
# Dooly
## /둘리/

<*Dooly* the Little Dinosaur> is a cartoon depicting the adventures of baby dinosaur *Dooly*, trapped in a glacier in the Ice Age and remaining frozen until awaking in modern Korea. He lives as a guest in the family house of Go Gil-dong, a resident of Ssangmun-dong, Seoul. The generation who grew up seeing this cartoon on TV are dubbed the "*Dooly* Generation".

Each year for the first decade since the first book was released in 1986, new instalments have been released, with a TV animation running since 1987. Beloved across the generations, it was remade in 2014 as an animated film for cinema release <The Great Invasion of Earth by the Preservative Girls>, while its *Webtoon* version was released in 2015 on Lezhin Comics, a paid *Webtoon* platform.[63]

Without doubt, it is one of the most popular in the history of Korean comics, and its native characters have been a commercial success, too. It has never been embroiled in plagiarism controversies, and it has won high acclaim for its unique drawing style, distinctive dinosaur protagonist, and reflection of issues in Korean society.

The series is continuously referenced in other media, including recent TV dramas. To give an example, since it is set in Ssangmun-dong, Seoul, it is much mentioned in the drama <Reply 1988> (TVN, 2015), where the action takes place in the same area – many of the characters and common locations are named after the *Dooly* series, for example "*Dooly* supermarket" and "*Ddochi* bistro", *Ddochi* being the name of *Dooly's* ostrich friend. Moreover, the nickname of protagonist, the Go player Choi Taek, is *Heedong*, which was the name of human baby from <*Dooly* the Little Dinosaur>. Meanwhile in the 2020 SBS drama <Penthouse>, the protagonist sang the theme song of *Dooly* with different lyrics.

## 36.
## Essence
## /에센스/

In K-Beauty, essence typically refers to a pre-toner product category. It used right after cleansing and before toner is applied. In practice, it is also possible to merge the two functions and to just choose an essence vs. a toner. The practice of a pre-toner essence can be traced back to the popularity of fermentation-based extracts that were popularised in its liquid form. Some brands formulate their pre-toner essences in light serum formulation and this can cause some confusion with users as to where in their routine to use it. Functionally, essences are a hydrating step.

# 37.
# Flower Boy
## /꽃보다 남자/

Literally meaning "flower handsome boy", the term gained popularity through films and drams such as <The King & The Clown> (2005) and <Boys over Flowers> (2009), and has been used to describe male characters who are handsome in a pretty box way in movies and dramas.

# 38.
# Friends
## /프렌즈/

One feature of Korean *Webtoons* is that they are serviced in conjunction with mobile messengers operated by web portal companies. Typical examples include "LINE" operated in Japan (by Naver) and "Kakao" in Korea. Against this background, several characters created to promote mobile messengers appear in identical form in *Webtoon* services. One example of this is the LINE Friends characters, born from an emoji sticker created for LINE mobile messenger in 2011. As the Korean *Webtoon* has become more popular and the market demand for *Webtoon* character goods has grown, the character merchandising business has expanded accordingly.

Drawing on know-how of developing LINE Friends, web portals partner with global companies such as Netflix, Tencent, and Big Hit Entertainment, to develop character goods for them, or collaboratively create new media, content starring the existing characters.[64]

# 39.
# Gaejeossi
## /개저씨/

Along similar lines to *altang* (see entry 6), the term used to criticise male-dominated films, some Korean net users call middle-aged characters *gaejeossi*, a mash-up of the word for "*ajeossi*" (아저씨; meaning middle-aged man) and the word "*gae*" (개; dog).

An offshoot of this term is "*gaejeo-BL*", which compounds BL (boy's love) and *gaejeossi*. It is used to refer sarcastically to the relationship between male characters when it unintendedly appears to be romantic. Both *gaejeossi* and *gaejeo-BL* are discriminatory terms against a specific age group, and care must be taken before use.

# 40.
# Gajok drama
## /가족 드라마/

As the name hints, this terms refers to TV dramas that air either in the evenings or on the weekends when *gajok* (가족; meaning family) can watch together. The aforementioned Korean terrestrial broadcasters tended to organise "*gajok* drama" during such times, and as they reminded people of family love [there was a] public perception that weekend drama is *gajok* drama. However, *jongpeon* (see entry 61) that were established in 2011 began to broadcast many *non-gajok* dramas on Friday and Saturday, undermining the unwritten rule.

Generally, the Korean Broadcasting System (KBS) has achieved high audience ratings for *gajok* dramas, giving birth to the phrase "the legend of the unbeatable KBS weekend drama".[65] As KBS is a public service broadcaster, their *gajok* dramas tend to advance the narratives in ways with which the South Korean population can generally sympathise, for example, family crises and conflicts between family members. Unlike "*makjang*" drama (low-quality television drama relying on inflammatory subject matters and rushed, unreasonable storylines; also see entry 69), *gajok* dramas often attempt to invoke emotion and understanding from audiences, portraying how family members unite to resolve crises and conflicts, how parents sacrifice and dedicate their lives to their children while children show "filial

**KOREAN DRAMA CHECKLIST**

1.
2.
3.
4.

piety" to their parents, and confirm their love for each other.

Some media scholars have pointed out that such Korean-style family drama can be considered KBS's response to the rapid individualisation and family deconstruction that followed the government bankruptcy in the late 1990s. According to this view, the broadcaster sought to reconstruct the imaginary of the traditional Korean family, restoring the idea of family and reminding audiences of notions of familial love and solidarity.[66]

# 41.
## Gaptuktui
## /갑툭튀/

An abbreviation of "*Gapjagi Tuk Teounaoda*" (갑자기 툭 튀어나오다), which means to suddenly burst. It is often used to describe a situation in a TV drama or movie where an unexpected character appears out of the blue and changes the situation.

# 42.
# Gochujang
## /고추장/

*Gochujang* is an original and unique condiment in Korea. As with China and Japan, Korea has long had a culture of using soybean paste in its cuisine. But during the Imjin War (Japanese invasions of Korea) in the 16th Century, chilli pepper ("*gochu*" in Korean) was introduced from Japan, and Koreans started developing an individual culture of making *gochujang* mainly with the pepper along with glutinous rice and "*meju*" (메주; a brick of dried fermented soybeans).[67]

The then-Korean diet was mostly vegetable-based, and the spiciness of red chilli peppers began to be in the limelight for working up the appetite, encouraging the development of various *gochujang*. Among the most famous is "*Sunchang gochujang*", known as a specialty of the Sunchang region. It is made around lunar July by mixing red chilli pepper powder made freshly from fresh red peppers, glutinous rice, and meju powders made from fermented soybeans. Renowned for its marvellous taste, it was loved by the Royal Family, and its recipe was even introduced in an 18th Century book.[68]

# 43.
# Gonali
## /고나리/

*Gonali* was originally a mistyped version of "*guanli*" (관리),[69] which in Korean means to manage or to supervise. However, it became widely used on the South Korean web as a word referring to know-it-all behaviours, or those who boss others around. A derivative of this is "*gonali-jil*", which with the suffix "*-jil*" which refers to demeaning activities or orders issued in a derogatory fashion.

# 44.
# Gongka
## /공카/

There are several different Korean terms that refer to a group of fans. First of them is "fandom", which is also used in other countries. Fandom is a compound word of "fan", which is itself a shortening of "fanatic", and the suffix "-dom", which means territory or country. It is used widely in K-Pop field to indicate people or a group of people who passionately support or revere celebrities or particular subject matter. On the other hand, *"gongka"* is abbreviation of *"gonsikjukin* fan café" (meaning the official fan café in Korean). While it also refers to a group of fans, there is a subtle difference between their exact meanings.

As the word "official" suggests, a *gongka* for a celebrity often plays a central role in organising and implementing various fan activities on behalf of the overall fandom, and as such, they sometimes communicate or liaise directly with the celebrity agencies.[70] They are also called "café" because they usually take on a form of "online café" (online communities) on large web portals, in which fans share photos and materials about their beloved celebrity and organise supporting activities.

Similarly, another term is *"fan-pa"* (팬페), a shortening of fan (web) pages. There are unofficial, so they are often managed by individuals, and take on formats ranging from social media to individual blog sites.

# 45.
## Gradation
### /그라데이션/

A term loaned from visual arts terminology,[71] the original concept refers to the technique of the gradual transitioning of colour, hue, shade and/or texture from one to another.[72] In a K-Beauty context, the technique has been most popularly applied to point makeup, especially in eye shadow and lip colour. In colloquial English, the term "gradient" would more likely be used to mean the same thing.

# 46.
# Gukppong
## /국뽕/

Gukppong is a neologism formed of "*guk*" (국; meaning *country*) and "*ppong*" (뽕; meaning *Hiroppong*, which is the Korean pronunciation of Philopon). Literally meaning "nation-meth", it refers to an ultranationalist state, where one is overly intoxicated with nationalism. Relatedly, "*gukppong* content" refer to the types of content and materials created to deliberately evoke such state, hence the ones that embody nationalist sentiment. For instance, a lot of *gukppong* content on Korean YouTube are entitled along the lines of "Overseas reactions to OO" or "Watch this to have *gukppong*" and tagged with "overseas reactions" or *gukppong*. As such, they deal with how much Korean pop culture is recognised in other countries.

Content of this kind present visual and auditory data to support their claims, or introduce reactions found in the user-created contents by non-Korean nationals, arguing that "you can take pride in being South Korean". In this regard, some experts point out that the rising popularity of these videos may be explained in relation to a desire to be recognised, or in light of the country's past colonial experience.[73] Meanwhile, increasing criticism has been levelled against the commercialisation of *gukppong* content, as some YouTubers are known to edit or fabricate overseas reactions to attract the viewers to earn advertising revenue.

# 47.
# Gwanjong
## /관종/

*Gwansim-jongja* is a newly-coined word that mashes up "*gwansim*" (관심; attention) and "*jongja*" (종자; one of a kind). Sometimes it is abbreviated as *gwanjong*. It is mainly used to negatively describe a person who acts or speaks out of a desire to draw attention from others.

# 48.
# Hallyu
## /한류/

A neologism coined to capture the increase in pan-Asian popularity of South Korean culture since the 1990s, in the form of pop music, entertainment, TV dramas, and the like.[74] In the case of pop music, it was launched in the 1990s by the then-popular boy band H.O.T, which was also admired in China. Since then, Korean boy and girl bands' dance music became widespread across Asia and beyond, popularising the term "K-Pop".

As for TV drama, in early 2000s several of the romantic dramas such as <Winter Sonata> (2002), <Dae Jang Geum> (2003), and <All In> (2003) were well received and widely popular in Japan and many Southeast Asian countries, contributing to the expansion of *hallyu*. Actors and actresses who starred in these dramas are called "*hallyu* stars". One of these stars, Bae Yong-joon, who starred in <Winter Sonata>, became exceptionally popular and admired among middle-aged women in Japan, and nicknamed as Yonsama.

More recently, South Korean TV dramas are streamed and watched outside Asia and widely in the US and Europe, via Netflix, while also being popular among younger generations.

# 49.
# Hoejeonmun
## /회전문/

The act of binge-reading *Webtoons*. Like going through the revolving door endlessly, it refers to reading from over and over again the *Webtoons* one has already finished reading from beginning to end.

# 50.
# Honbab
## /혼밥/

A portmanteau of the Korean words for "*hon[ja]*" (혼자; meaning alone) and "*bab*" (밥; rice). Here, rice is used in Korean to refer to food in general. One of the latest phenomena in Korean society is that ordinary people prefer eating along to eating together with colleagues or family members, for different reasons.[75]

With the increase of people living alone throughout big cities, the traditional culture of sharing food with family members has disappeared, and the "*honbab* culture" has begun to develop over the last decade. The increasing popularity of convenient/fast food such as a lunch boxes that can be bought at a 24-hour convenience store and the night-time food delivery service where ordering and payment are performed through a mobile phone application, have supported the development of this culture.[76]

# 51.
## Honey butter
### /허니버터/

As the name suggests, "honey butter" sauces are made of sweet honey and savoury butter, and honey butter-based foods and snacks have been popular in South Korea since the mid-2000s. The trend is believed to have begun in 2004 when Eun-hee Kim, the CEO of Korean coffee franchise "Coffine Grunaru", developed honey butter bread.[77] Then in 2014, Japanese snack maker "Calbee" and Korean snack maker "Haitai" collaboratively created a snack called "Honey butter chip", and it was a massive hit in South Korea that it experienced a great shortage for a while.

    The latest hit in this line of trend is "Honey butter almond", developed by a medium-sized firm Gilim corporation, inspired by the Honey butter chip. Its gross profit in the first two months of sale was 1.5 billion Korean Won (approximately 1.3 million USD). Since its success, Gilim developed more than more than 20 different flavoured almonds, such as wasabi, cookie and cream, tiramisu, seaweed, and starlight pangpang flavours. Their annual export total 9,000 tons to 16 different countries, and their revenue for 2014 almost doubled from 64.9 billion Korean Won (approximately 58 million USD) to 139.6 billion Korean Won (approximately 124 million USD).[78]

    On the Korean Web, the success of honey butter-based products is sometimes dubbed as "the victory of *dan-jjan*". "*Dan-jjan*" is a neologism popular since the mid 2010 as a mash-up of "*dan*" (단; sweet) and "*jjan*" (짠; salty/savoury).[79] It is known as an "unfailing cooking rule" as the combination of sweet and savoury saltiness enhances the overall flavour.

South Korea's love for "honey butter" flavour traces back to 2004 when Kim Eun-hee, a Korean businesswoman who later founded the Korean coffee chain Coffine Gurunaru, first developed the recipe for "Honey butter bread"; then, the honey butter "craze" began in 2014 when the Haitai Confectionery and Foods released "Honey butter chips". Following the success of Honey butter chips in the country, a variety of snacks and nuts in honey butter flavour were soon launched to capitalise on the trend.

## 52.
## Hot Chicken
## /불닭/

When it was first launched in 2012, few predicted that Hot Chicken Flavour Ramen ("*buldak-bokkeum-myeon*" in Korean) would become such a popular ramen, even being widely exported overseas. It used to be considered a product that would appeal only to a small number of hot spice enthusiasts, as it was too hot and spicy even for Korean tastes. However, around 2016, the situation changed sharply as *buldak-bokkeum-myeon* challenges began on YouTube.[80] As the number of YouTubers either introducing Korean culture or streaming live eating increased, they also started taking on the challenge of consuming this incredibly spicy and tongue-numbing noodle as fast as possible, contributing to the challenge going viral.

YouTube video clips tagged with "Hot Chicken Flavour Ramen" or "Fire Noodle Challenge" were widely circulated online, attracting the attention of overseas mass media. In turn, Samyang Food, the producer of the ramen, capitalised on the trend, developing various different flavoured ramens, such as Hot Chicken "Cheese" Flavour, Hot Chicken "Mala" Flavour, and Hot Chicken "Carbonara" Flavour, with a view to boost the challenges further.[81] As the interest in Korean pop culture increased along with *Hallyu* (see entry 48), so did the interest in this ramen among those who wanted to try quick, easy-to-cook Korean food. Therefore, it is no exaggeration that all Korean or Asian supermarkets overseas stock *buldak-bokkeum-myeon*; it is even sold on Amazon and eBay.

# 53.
## Idol
## /아이돌/

As in the Anglo-American music world, the word "idol" in South Korea is used to refer to those who are admired or loved by their fans. However, while the word is used in the West for stars in the extensive fields, from film and pop music to sports, in the South Korean context, it is almost exclusively used to indicate K-Pop boy and girl bands, most of whose members are in their late 10s and early 20s. Since the legendary trio "Seo Taiji and Boys" in the 1990s, modern pop music has become the mainstream in the South Korean music scene, laying the foundations on which so-called "idol bands" emerged.[82] These idol bands are popular not only among teenagers and adolescents, but also those in their 30s and 40s ("uncle fans" or "aunt fans"), thereby forming a socially seminal group of artists.

One of the frontrunners among these bands is the BTS, who recently entered the British and American music scene. They are considered as a successful example of exported Korean pop culture, and their music is regarded as important evidence of the expansion of South Korean soft power, represented by the Korean Wave.

At the same time, however, there has also been a backlash to this commercialisation of Korean pop culture. One of the criticisms levelled is against the standardised style of their songs, in the form of fast-beat dance music

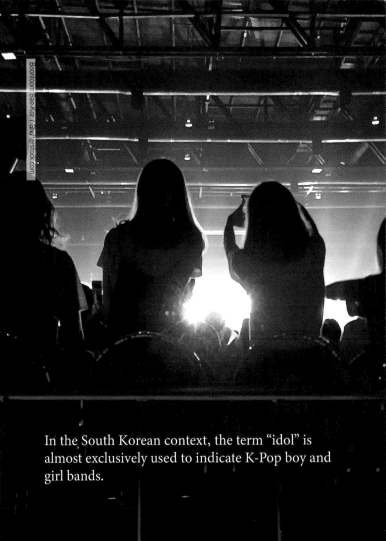

In the South Korean context, the term "idol" is almost exclusively used to indicate K-Pop boy and girl bands.

combined with vibrant and showy dancing performance (a.k.a. "*gun-mu*" (군무), meaning group dancing perfectly in sync). In this regard, some find the reason for such standardisation of idol music and the focus on dance music from the division of labour in music production.[83] For instance, one of the largest entertainment companies in South Korea, SM Entertainment, first introduced this division of labour system, comprising various sectors in management, production, visuals, marketing, IT, and management support, with a view to optimising the process of music creation. Moreover, production itself is divided into several parts, in charge of domestic and overseas A&R, casting, training, and so on. Members of idol bands are even assigned different roles from the outset, for example main vocal, lead vocal, main dancer, entertainer, and so on. While such efforts may help to secure greater diversity among individual band members, orchestrating such diversity inevitably requires the band to take on dance music genres.

On the other hand, sexual commodification is a problem that has been broadly highlighted. One particular criticism that has been raised is with regards to the commodification and marketing strategies of entertainment companies that often aim to maximise the sexual charm of idol bands, even though most members are still teenagers or in their early 20s. Kim Soo-ah (2011) critically discussed the case of girl idols, analysing the PR images of girl bands, showing how entertainment companies and agencies exploit erotic dances and seductive costumes as a strategy to maximise sexuality and increase profitability.[84]

However, some later works by other scholars have

pointed out that, more recently, girl groups are working to reform their public image in ways that do not overly appeal to sexuality, and instead wear less revealing outfits or more girly chiffon and lace dresses.[85] This is due to the fact that girl idols are becoming popular not only among teenagers and boys but also across all generations and genders, so the idol culture as a whole has become the mainstream in the Korean pop music scene. Of course, this may still be understood not as the disappearance of sexualisation of idols, but rather as the diversification of commodification of idol bands, as the size of industry has grown.

# 54.
# Ilbe
# /일베/

An abbreviation of "*Ilgan-best* storehouse", a far-right populist online community derived from another community DC Inside and founded in April 2010.[86] Ilbe has been reported on by the mass media several times and is widely known for its extreme abhorrence of liberal politicians and antagonistic stance against feminism, Jeolla province, and LGBTQ+ movements. With regards to feminism in particular, Ilbe have continuously claimed that men are the underdog in South Korean society, and it is believed that many online feminist movements began as a backlash against Ilbe.[87]

# 55.
## Ilko
### /일코/

A shortening of "*ilban-in* cosplay", which is itself a mash-up of "*ilban-in*" (meaning ordinary people) and "*cosplay*", a Japanese portmanteau of "costume play" referring to activities in which participants wear costumes and fashion accessories to represent a specific character from manga or anime. Generally, it denotes hiding their fondness for a celebrity being conscious of the gaze around them. A derivative of Ilko is "*ilko haejae*" (일코 해제), which means to stop *ilko*.

# 56.
# Ilsangtoon
## /일상툰/

A considerable number of entries into *Webtoon* platforms take the form of so-called "*Ilsangtoon*", or daily life cartoons. Several of the amateur cartoonists who produce *Webtoons* are eager to tell their own story, for instance combining self-narration and comical expressions. Indeed, sometimes it is considered more convenient to make daily life cartoons than genre-specific cartoons when it comes to serialisation. Since the cartoonists themselves appear as a character in this instance, they act out their own lives in the cartoons.[88]

# 57.
# Inbyul
## /인별/

On the Korean web, non-Korean social media platforms are sometimes given Korean nicknames. For example, Facebook is called "*Eolgul-chek*", where "*eolgul*" (얼굴) means face and "*chek*" (책) book. Similarly, Instagram is referred to as "*Inbyulgram*", or more simply "*Inbyul*", with "*byul*" (별) meaning star in Korean.

# 58.
# Insam
# /인삼/

To help differentiate it from ginseng from other countries, Korean ginseng is called "*Goryeo Insam*", or Korean ginseng. This has been true since as far back as the Goryeo dynasty. In Sino-Korean characters, ginseng is written as "蔘", while foreign ginsengs are written "參", a tradition which has continued to the present time.[89] Ginseng has been used as a rejuvenating medicine for thousands of years, thanks to its effect of improving immunity and tackling fatigue.[90] In particular, steamed and dried Korean ginseng are beloved by Korean people as "*hongsam*" (홍삼; red ginseng), thanks to the reddish colour it takes on. It is also gaining reputation as a must-buy gift among tourists visiting South Korea.

# 59.
## Inso
## /인소/

In South Korean society in the 2000s, Internet (based) literature (also known as Internet novels, or "*Inso*" for short) became popular among teenagers who grew up on the Internet and had been baptised in popular culture. *Inso* actively used Internet slang, wonky grammatical structures, and an excessive range of emoticons, all of which were considered taboo not only in the pure literature but even popular novels at the time, thereby causing controversy about whether *inso* should be considered as literature.[91] In the end, its light and cheerful touch with regards to romantic love among teenagers was rewarded with huge commercial success.

Among *inso* writers, one of the most famous was "Guiyeoni" (the pen name of Lee Yoon-sae). Her novels <He was Cool> (2001), <Temptation of Wolves> (2002), and <Do Re Mi Fa So La Ti Do> (2003) were a great commercial hit, leading to what was known as "Guiyeoni syndrome".[92] All three works were printed in paperback, and even adapted into films. In particular, the 2004 film <Temptation of Wolves> helped Gang Dong-won, a then-unknown actor, gain overnight fame, especially for the scene where he appeared under the heroine's umbrella showing his foxy smile.

Internet novels were once thought to be a fleeting trend, yet they entered a second heyday with the rise of Internet-novel-specialised platforms such as Munpia and

Joara, and then with the provision by such large portals as Naver and Kakao (formerly Daum) of platforms that supported the sustained and professional production and consumption of amateur novels.

The difference between *inso* and current amateur novels (often referred to as "web novels") is that the former became popular on the Web and then published in print, whereas the latter are published and consumed on digital platforms. Consumers of web novels use apps on their smart devices to read the novels, based on either pay-per-view or subscription, via fintech payments. Generally, an episode costs 100 KRW (US 10c).[93] Thanks to the introduction of such "pay per view" options, amateur writers have gained greater financial stability, resulting in the further growth of the writer pool.

Meanwhile, like Internet novels, web novels are being adapted into films and TV dramas, as an important part of the media mix in the South Korean cultural industry. This is in line with the "one source multi-use" strategy, a key trend in Korea since 2000, where a single piece of source material gives rise to a whole variety of cultural items – ranging from Webtoon, web novels, game, to films and TV dramas.[94]

# 60.
## Jisangpa
## /지상파/

Technically, South Korean broadcasting services comprise *jisangpa*, cable, and satellite broadcasting. "*Jisangpa*" is a term referring to terrestrial television and radio broadcasting services, for which the signal is transmitted by broadcasting waves from the terrestrial (Earth-based) transmitter of a television station to a TV receiver. Meanwhile, cable and satellite broadcasting use signals transmitted through electronic or fibre-optic cables and satellites, respectively. However, South Korean people tend to use *jisangpa* to refer to the TV broadcasts in general. South Korean *jisangpa* include public-funded broadcasters KBS and MBC, and commercially funded broadcaster SBS.

# 61.
## Jjaekjjaegi
*/짹짹이/*

While "*Eolgul-chek*" and "*Inbyul*" are Korean nicknames for Facebook and Instagram (see entry 57), the nickname for Twitter is "*Jjaekjjaegi*". This word is mostly used among K-Pop fandom and the Korean equivalent for the verb "to twitter", or a bird's chirp, is "*jjaek jjaek*", which combined with the noun suffix "*-i*", gives *Jjaekjjaegi*.

# 62.
# Jogong
## /조공/

The dictionary meaning of "*jogong*" (tribute in Korean) is the tribute or gifts paid periodically by one state or ruler to another as a sign of dependence. In K-Pop fandom, however, it is a term that refers to individual and collective sending of gifts to idol singers to express affection. Usually, fan communities fundraise over certain periods of time, and the management of the communities buy gifts and send them on behalf of fans to the agencies of idol singers. A related expression is "carrying the ball", which refers to taking the initiative in fan activities.[95] Some see such distinctive gifting activities in K-Pop culture as a fun, productive, hands-on form of "consumer participation".[96] However, there is a risk that these gifting activities might render the relationship between fans and the stars more asymmetrical, as the original meaning of *jogong* implies.

Relatedly, from another negative standpoint, several media outlets have pointed out the lists of gifts made by different fandoms are often compared with one another online, fuelling competition between the fandoms and eventually leading to the gifts becoming luxury items, designer clothes and accessories, contributing to rendering the *jogong* as a showing-off culture. Several fandoms are increasingly aware of such critique, and so recently have started replacing large fractions of *jogong* with acts of "goodwill" instead, making donations to charities and not-for-profit organisations and volunteering for the social goods, with a view to lowering the negative public perception towards *jogong*. In particular, K-Pop bands such as BTS, NU'EST, and Seventeen have publicly announced that they will refuse any gifts other than handwritten letters from fans, so their fandoms tend to focus more on charitable activities.[97]

## Yeok-jogong (역조공)

In K-Pop culture, "*jogong*" is used as a slang for fans sending gifts to idol singers to express their affection. "*Yeok-jogong*", where the prefix "*yeok*" means "contrary", therefore means the opposite, and is widely used in K-Pop fandom to describe K-Pop bands or idol singers giving gifts to their fans. For instance, BTS, Hyuna, Suzy, and IU offer fans at their concert or fan meetings such gifts as: "*dosirak*" (도시락; packed meals and snacks), clothes and cosmetics (in the case of Hyuna); goods from the brands for which they model (in the case of Suzy); T-shirts or photo cards with their names or photos on (in the case of BTS Suga); and rings to commemorate the 10th anniversary of their debut (IU).[98]

# 63.
## Jongpeon
## /종편/

Historically, the broadcasting industry in South Korea has been dominated by older terrestrial broadcasters, but as the revised "Newspaper Act and the Broadcasting Act" were legislated on 22nd July 2009, new competitors started to emerge.[99] This amendment has permitted newspaper companies to operate a broadcasting corporation, and relaxed the regulations around private sector ownership of broadcasting corporations. As a result, three major newspapers in South Korea – JoongAng Ilbo, Chosun Ilbo, and Dong-a Ilbo –established JTBS, TV Chosun, and Channel A. These channels are referred to as "*Jongpeon*", an abbreviation in Korean of "*Jonghap Peonsung* Channel", meaning a channel that runs programmes in all manner of genres, ranging from news reporting and entertainment, to drama and documentary.

# 64.
# Jopok
# /조폭/

Jopok is short for "*Jojik Pokryeokbae*" (조직폭력배), which refers to the gangsters of South Korea. Beginning with the film <Friend> in 2001, a number of films and dramas featuring *jopok* began to enter the mainstream. <Friend> is a narrative about *jopok* who had been childhood friends but were going through a tough time. The film popularised several Gyeongsang-do expressions, including "*Chin-gu aiga*" ("Aren't We Friends") and "*Chin-gu kiri mian hal gut oepta*" ("No Need for Friends to Say Sorry"). Since the success of <Friend>, many films featuring and appropriating jopok have been produced. Examples include <Kick The Moon> (2001), <My Wife Is Gangster> (2001), <Let's Play, Dharma> (2001), <Marrying the Mafia> (2002), <A Bittersweet Life> (2005), <Sunflower> (2006), <A Dirty Carnival> (2006), <My Boss, My Hero> (2006), <The Show Must Go On> (2007), <New World> (2013), <Gangnam Blues> (2015) and <Coin Locker Girl> (2015), to name just a few.

Typically, these films are based on bloody struggles for money that bring about a crisis in protagonists bound by brotherhood or friendship. Although it may be positively interpreted as a critique of the brutality of a society replete with materialism and mammonism, some critics voice the criticism that most Korean gangster films do not focus enough on the brutal aspects of gangsterism, unlike the

Hollywood films that portray various forms of retribution and the tragic fall of gangsters who rely on violence.[100]

# 65.
## Joseon zombie
### /조선 좀비/

Following on from the success of Netflix Original Korean drama <Kingdom> (2019), zombie films set in the Joseon dynasty and the accompanying "Joseon zombies" have attracted widespread attention in the South Korean broadcasting industry. The pioneer of this trend, <Kingdom> set against the backdrop of a sanguinary royal feud, tells the story of a crown prince in the Joseon dynasty who struggles to save people from turning into zombies following a plague of unknown cause, and who grows into a true heir to the throne. Upon release, it went viral globally thanks to its unique content, and received critical acclaim for the strong performance of the lead actors and actresses, its enthralling bow and sword fighting, and the artistic expression of the "*hanbok*" (한복; Korean traditional clothing) and "*gat*" (갓; traditional Korean hat) that were integral to the Joseon period. As of 29th April 2021, <Kingdom> had gained a 96% "Fresh" rating on film review-aggregation site Rotten Tomatoes, considered highly positive.[101] Meanwhile, the same year saw the release of another Joseon zombie film <Rampant> (2018), which was simultaneously adapted into a popular *Webtoon*. Together, they are often referred to as the "*Joseon* zombie" series.

In the years that followed these early hits, similar works have been produced, for example <Joseon Exorcist>

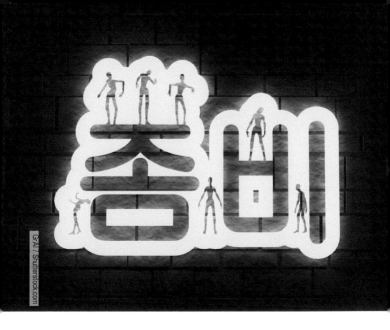

(2021) which was aired on SBS but cancelled after just two episodes. This drama featured an idiosyncratic plot where in a Joseon kingdom that was being devasted by a "*saeng-si*" (생시; a zombie + demon like evil creature), two kings Taejong and Grand Prince Chungnyeong (later Sejong the Great) took on the task of exorcising the demon, with assistance from a Roman Catholic priest. The drama was produced with budget of 32 billion KRW (approximately $28.5 million). However, its use of Chinese-style props depicting foods, clothes, and architecture did not sit well with the viewers, and the suspected distortion of historical facts around the two kings caused further controversy, leading to the cancellation of the drama.[102]

# 66.
## K-Pop
### /케이팝/

In general, K-Pop evokes a genre of music designed to be enjoyed visually as much as aurally, with songs using "hooks" with upbeat rhythms and fast beats that are easy to sing along to and choreograph, with colourful makeup and costumes – "*gunmu*" (군무) in K-Pop refers to group dancing perfectly in sync. Given these attributes, it is no coincidence that K-Pop became known to overseas audiences through video sharing site YouTube. Although K-Pop was inspired by Western pop genres and its lyrics contain a lot of English language, many academics consider K-Pop a cultural "hybridisation" rather than a pure assimilation,[103] not least because it captures and delivers Korean cultural meaning and sentiments through Korean-language lyrics.

In terms of its fandom, K-Pop is considered to have the largest overseas fan base among *Hallyu* or K-Culture genres,[104] with a fandom that tends to expand naturally in the process of communicating with others from different cultural and national backgrounds – for instance, through the comments on music videos and songs on YouTube and social media such as Facebook and Twitter. As this global K-Pop fandom is formed through the communication among platform users, transcending nationalities, it observes the formation of a "transculture" that overcomes cultural differences.[105]

An example of K-Pop concert – the boy band "2PM" on the stage at the Human Culture Equilibrium Concert Korea Festival in Vietnam on March 22, 2014.

# 67.
## KFC
## /치킨/

A shortening of "Korean Fried Chicken". In fact, this term is not used in Korea; instead, Koreans use the term "*chikin*" (adapted pronunciation of chicken) to refer to a variety of deep-fried chicken dishes. It is worth noting that behind the background of the popularity of chicken in Korean society lie unique social and cultural circumstances.

In more detail, as the country went through several financial crises, those who had voluntarily retired became self-employed, and started to run fried chicken shops, as this was something that did not require sophisticated culinary skills. 24 hour and night-time delivery services increased and competition intensified with the mass entry of new markets suppliers. By 2014, the fast-growing Korean late-night meal market was estimated at 10-15 trillion Korean won, 12-19% of the total food service market,[106] with chicken revealed as one of the favourite night-time delivery dishes.[107] Interestingly, approximately 50% of total order volumes came from the period between 8pm and 4am. In 2013, there were 22,529 franchise-based fried chicken restaurants in the country, including over 30,000 independently-owned fried chicken stores or local bars selling fried chicken. For reference, in the same year, the number of McDonald's stores was 35,429 globally.[108]

Korean "chicken", which is renowned for its sweet

and spicy flavour, seasoned with hot pepper paste and sugar, has seen soaring popularity in overseas sales thanks to the demand from foreign audiences curious about the food that appears so frequently in K-Dramas. According to the article "South Korea's Fried Chicken Craze Sparks Battle for Market Share" in <Fortune> (2016), exports to East Asia have increased sharply from the early 2000s.[109]

becky's / Shutterstock.com

"KFC" (Korean Fried Chicken) is renowned for its sweet and spicy flavour, seasoned with hot pepper paste and sugar.

# 68.
# Kimchi
# /김치/

*Kimchi* is a type of food made with Korea's unique fermentation technology, developed along with attempts to pickle vegetables to store them for a long time. Unlike the acetic acid storage method, in which vegetables are dried or cooked and then sterilised with liqueur or vinegar, raw vegetables are salted and seasoned to make *kimchi*. It is also differentiated from other pickled vegetables in that it is fermented in "*onggi*" (옹기), large earthenware vessels unique to Korea.[110]

*Kimchi* originates from the Three Kingdoms period (57 BC to 668 AD), and unsurprising given its long history, many recipes exist today. Different provinces in Korea use varying ingredients, and more than 300 recipe variations have been recorded. Arguably, the best known is "*baechu kimchi*" (배추김치), made with napa cabbage marinated with red chilli pepper powder, even though its history is relatively short, as it began to be made in the times of the Joseon Dynasty, around the 16th Century.[111]

These days, *kimchi* is well known globally as a traditional Korean food. On 5th December 2013, <*Kimjang*: Making and Sharing *Kimchi* in the Republic of Korea>, was inscribed on the UNESCO's Representative List of the Intangible Cultural Heritage of Humanity. "*Kimjang*" (김장) refers to the making practice of *kimchi*, and is introduced by

UNESCO as a "collective practice . . . [which] reaffirms Korean identity and offers excellent opportunities for strengthening family cooperation".[112]

In 2001, *kimchi* acquired the international food standard of the International Food Standards Committee (Codex), a reference point which has since been recognised as the international standard for pickled products bearing the name *kimchi*. Codex means "code" in Latin, and the Codex is the international guideline and code of practice for food, established by the Food and Agriculture Organization (FAO) and World Health Organization (WHO).[113]

The first commercial kimchi brand in South Korea was Doosan's Jonggajip, launched in December 1987. In recent years, as *kimchi* has been found to have many health benefits, and as an excellent probiotic fermented food, overseas exports have increased, even to the point where American monthly magazine <Health> described *kimchi* as one of the world's five healthiest foods.[114] This has encouraged other food companies including CJ Bibigo to start kimchi businesses, and *kimchi*'s popularity has soared even more lately, as the global interest in fermented foods' ability to activate the immune system has increased, not least against the backdrop of COVID-19. From January to August in 2020, for example, the export value of *kimchi* recorded 97.9 million USD, a 40.3% increase on the previous year.[115]

Arguably, the best known *kimchi* is *"baechu kimchi"* (배추김치), made with napa cabbage marinated with red chilli pepper powder.

# 69.
## Korean heart
### /손가락 하트/

The finger heart is a gesture crossing the thumb and index finger of one hand to form a heart shape. Opinions are divided as to where it originated. Nam Woo-hyun, a member of a K-Pop idol band Infinite, is often considered the first person to have made the gesture, as it came to be popularised in 2013, around the time Woohyun started using it to address his fans. Others have pointed out that Buzz's Min Kyung-hoon and BIGBANG's G-Dragon were photographed making the finger heart sign earlier, however, suggesting they proceeded Nam Woo-hyun.[116]

# 70.
# Laenseon
## /랜선/

An online trend exists in Korea of using "LAN cable" (the ethernet cable plugged into a PC for Internet use) as a suffix. In case of *Webtoons*, this is most often used in daily life cartoons based on babies or animal companions; many audiences call themselves LAN cable aunts (*imo*) and uncles (*samchon*) for babies and animal companions.

# 71.
# Makgeolli
## /막걸리/

The etymology of *makgeolli* is "*mak geolluseo mashin sul*" (막 걸러서 마신 술; alcohol that has just been strained and drunk). "*Mak geolluda*" means filtering or straining by putting alcohol in a sieve and pressing with the hands, or stirring with a spatula. Unlike bitter-tasting alcohol made by carefully squeezing grains, these the freshly filtered alcohol has a relatively mild taste.[117]

Because of its cloudy appearance that seems to be a mixture of water and grain flour, it is classified as "*takju*" (탁주) - where "*tak*" means cloudy or opaque, and "*ju*" alcohol. In the past, *takju* was made from the leftovers of "*cheongj*" (청주) making. In Korea, *cheongju* generally refers to clear alcohol ladled out of the fermented rice wine. Then, *makgeolli* used to be made with the leftover "*jigemi*" (지게미; lees), filtering the remaining rice wine.[118]

Although *makgeolli* is not well known overseas, in Korea it is widely loved by ordinary people for its relatively cheap price compared to *cheongju*. There are several famous *makgeolli* brands, such as "*Jangsu makgeolli*" in Seoul,[119] "*Saengtag makgeolli*" in Busan,[120] and "*Ildong makgeolli*" in Pocheon.[121] More recently, younger generations have been consuming *makgeolli* in more diverse ways, such as by adding fruit elements, mixing with other ingredients to make cocktails, or making "*makgeolli* bread" made by steaming fermented dough made from *makgeolli*.[122]

# 72.
# Makjang
## /막장/

The word *makjang*, in dictionary terms, is "a blind end [front] in a mine gallery", or the dead end of a tunnel.[123] More recently, it has been used to refer to someone whose misbehaviour ends up resulting in the worst situation, or simply to someone's wrongdoings. For example, "*makjang* drama" indicates low-quality television drama whose inflammatory narratives and implausible storylines provoke anger from the audience.

# 73.
# Manager mum
## /매니저 엄마/

In many Korean dramas and films, the role of mums is often that of educational managers who organise their children's private education activities. One good example of this is the characters in <SKY Castle>.[124] This is a 2018 South Korean television series (available on Netflix), where the title refers dually to the lives of housewives living in a luxurious residence called "SKY Castle", and to the acronym of the top 3 universities in South Korea (Seoul, Korea, and Yonsei University). It has become one of the highest-rating dramas in Korean cable television's history, thanks to its intriguing portrayal of two intertwining narratives: how competition among upper-class housewives in the contemporary South Korea leads to competition between children's private education and the university entrance examination, and the unravelling of a murder mystery in the midst of their luxurious surroundings.

# 74.
# Maneul
## /마늘/

The Korea's country founding myth tells the story of a bear who turned into a human being after eating "garlic". The following is an excerpt from the myth, taken from the <Chosun Ilbo for kids> column[125]: "A long time ago, Hwanung, the son of Heaven, ruled the people. There lived a tiger and a bear that wished to become humans, so they prayed every day to Hwanung. Hwanung called them and gave them garlic and mugwort, saying 'You can become human if you eat only garlic and mugwort for 100 days in a dark cave.' The tiger gave up after a little while, but the bear stayed in a cave alone. Surprisingly, after 21 days, she turned into a beautiful woman. Hwanung took her as his wife and she gave birth to a son. They named him Dangun. He grew up and established a country, Gojoseon. It was the first kingdom of Korean history".

Traditionally, in Korean society garlic and mugwort have been regarded as magical plants that repel demons and cleanse impurities. In the above story, garlic symbolises the "persistence" required to achieve one's goals, and it is used as a cultural symbol to show the identity of Korean people as marked by "self-control".[126] Garlic is used widely in Korean food today. In particular, it is an essential ingredient for *kimchi*.

# 75.
# Mandu
## /만두/

*Mandu* is a general term for dumplings in Korea. "Bibigo *Mandu*", launched by the South Korea's largest food company CJ Foods, is consumed extensively around the world, recording sales of 1 trillion KRW (approximately 0.9 billion USD) in 2020 alone. 65% of the revenue comes from overseas exports, and it sells especially well in the United States, where it even exceeds domestic sales.[127] According to analysis of Korean media outlets, the secret of this popularity is owing to a CJ Foods' marketing strategy that differentiates mandu as a healthy food from other dumplings, emphasising how "Bibigo *mandu*" are full of vegetables wrapped inside a thin dumpling skin, as opposed to Chinese dumplings with thicker skin and more meaty fillings.[128]

# 76.
# Minari
## /미나리/

Water parsley [celery], the word *minari* has a long history, stretching back unchanged to the 15th Century. According to the Encyclopaedia of Korean Culture, the word appears in the "Korea History" of the Goryeo Dynasty.[129]

*Minari* has a distinctive flavour and is generally eaten boiled or blanched and seasoned, although sometimes it is added raw to *kimchi*, to add freshness. Sometimes, it is also added as an herb to dishes like steamed fish and pork or soup, to help remove strong odours.

*Minari* has become beloved in Korea, partly because it is easy to cultivate even in a barren environment and climate, thanks to its strong vitality. For this reason, in a namesake 2020 film produced in the USA, minari appears as a medium that contributes to the bond of a Korean immigrant family struggling to settle in Arkansas. Isaac Jung, the director of the film, revealed that he was impressed how the *minari* seeds that his grandmother brought in grew well in Arkansas, and therefore decided to develop a story of immigrant family akin to the "tough vitality and adaptability of minari".[130] Youn Yuh-jung, who played the role of grandmother Sun-ja in the film, often seen planting *minari*, won Best Supporting Actress at the 2021 Oscars.

*

## Parasite, before Minari...

Sometimes, <Minari> is compared to Bong Joon-ho's <Parasite>, which won four awards in last year's Oscar's, including the Best Picture, Best Director, Best Original Screenplay, and Best International Feature Film.

What these two films have in common is that they were written and directed by Korean-born directors, Lee Isaac Chung and Bong Joon-ho. For this reason, Korean language is used in both films, and they are often categorised as foreign language films. In fact, both won the Golden Globe Award for Best Foreign Language Film. At the same time, however, there are differences between the two films in terms of genre, theme and production systems. As mentioned, Lee Isaac Chung is a Korean-born immigrant who was educated in the United States, and he portrayed the hardships of a Korean immigrant family chasing the American dream. This is a topic that can evoke sympathy generally within the multiracial American society. The film was also produced by Plan B Entertainment, owned by Brad Pitt.

Conversely, Bong Joon-ho's <Parasite> depicts how the poor Kim family – starting with the son, then the daughter, and then the whole family – has come to parasitise the wealthy Park family, through a series of lies they tell. Parasite, the title of the film, is a term that is commonly used in the South Korean society to refer derogatorily to those who live off others without making efforts themselves – just the parasites that live on people or livestock. In this case, the symbiotic relationship established between the two families eventually comes to a devastating end, as the Kims' poverty remains unresolved (despite their uncontrollable and increasing greed) and a secret in the Parks' house is revealed.

Mixing genres including thriller, satire and horror, Bong Joon-ho carefully tackles sensitive social issues such as the class and wealth gap between rich and the poor, in a story that seems "simple" at first glance. As these are issues universally found in any capitalist society, <Parasite> drew a great deal of sympathy in other cultures and societies, even though it is a Korean-language film whose set in Korea and performed only by Korean actors. In the end, the film became the first non-English-language film with an entirely Asian cast to win the Oscar for Best Picture.[131]

# 77.
# Minpye
## /민폐/

In Korean dictionaries, *minpye* is defined as "harm (to the public)". In films and TV drama, it is usually used as a modifier for characters who appear out of the blue and ruin the good work of the protagonists. Yet sometimes the protagonist is also critiqued for being a *minpye* character. For example, Eonnyeon, the female protagonist of the drama <Chuno>, earned criticism from audiences for the way she continuously brought the male protagonist Daegil into crisis, and only dealt passively with crisis, while shamelessly receiving assistance from those around her. During the airing of the drama, even a "*minpye* list of Eonnyeon" was created and popularised on the Korean Web.[132] *Minpye* is sometimes compounded with the word "*makjang*" (see entry 69), and the term "*minpye-makjang-nyeo*" is used to refer to a female character who always gets her own way, despite damaging the lives of others.

In conjunction with this, some critics have sought to find reasons for the emergence in Korean films and dramas of such minpye and *makjang* characters, especially female ones. One theory is that this is due to a lack of context or backstory, sacrificed at the expense of advancing and speeding up the plot, leading to characters appearing disrespectful and annoying, contrary to producers' intentions. Another is that sometimes women are obliged to play a passive role while male protagonists serve as problem-solvers. Expressing clear frustration at this trope, one renowned actress Ajoong Kim complained in a media interview that "it is a shame many female characters are often drawn into roles limited to the purely sexual, or simply makes themselves nuisance so male protagonists can come and resolve things".[133]

# 78.
# Muggle
## /머글/

Muggle is a term used by wizards and witches in J. K. Rowling's <Harry Potter> novels (1997-2007), to refer to an ordinary person not aware of the world of magic and lacking any sort of magical capability. As the novel became popular around the world, in 2002 the word entered the Oxford English Dictionary, denoting "a person who lacks a particular skill or skills, or who is regarded as inferior in some way".[134] In the South Korean context, however, muggle is used to distinguish between a fan who is loyal to a celebrity (mostly idol singers), like *deokhu* (see entry 32), and those who are not. Hence, muggle refers to those who do not *deok-jil*, who are not a fan of an idol singer. One derivative of muggle is "muggle king", which refers to a particular member of idol bands who even seduces ordinary people and turns them into *deokhu*. Normally, they are those members of an idol band who are most popular and widely known, with the most prominent profile. "Muggle king" is sometimes used interchangeably with "sales king", as they are good at "selling" themselves to muggles, converting them to fandom. For example, the newspaper "Korean Sports Business" referenced EXO's Xiumin, BTS's V and Astro's Cha Eun-woo as chief muggle kings.[135]

# 79.
# Mukbang
# /먹방/

Etymologically, the word *Mukbang* is a compound of two Korean words "*mukneun*" (먹는; meaning eating) and "*bangsong*" (방송; broadcast). Since South Korean live streaming platform Afreeca TV launched its service in 2005, *Mukbang* has attracted attention among audiences as a short live video showing BJs (short for Broadcasting Jockeys) eating different kinds of food in front of a Webcam, soon becoming one of the most popular genres on the platform. The mainstream media in South Korea started to pay attention to the use of the term a while later, when it was mentioned as a buzzword for the first time in a <Hankuk Ilbo> article of 2009.[136]

*Mukbang* is also distinguished from cooking content in print media such as newspapers and magazines, which tend to describe in detail the art of cooking while using (usually healthy) ingredients and showing professional criticism and commentary on the recipe. It is also differentiated from those programmes dealing with over-indulgence of food or eating competitions such as the ESPN's infamous <Nathan's Hot Dog Eating Contest>, as it entails not only real-time streaming, but also live social interactions with the audiences during streaming.

# 80.
# Mulgwang
# /물광/

Directly translates as "water shine". This is an extension of the skin condition described under "*chokchok*" (see entry 24). The concept of *mulgwang* is used in both skincare and makeup, and a skin that has achieved mulgwang is conceptually able to reflect light like a liquid pool of water, as it is so even in texture and hydration. There is a visible moistness in the concept in *mulgwang* that is not evident in *chok chok* skin, and in makeup terms, the concept is delivered through the use of moist formulas and liquid point makeup.

Equivalents in other East Asian beauty concepts include *tsuyadama* (つや玉) in Japanese and the more general phrase *guangzé* (光澤) in Mandarin.

# 81.
# Naelonambul
## /내로남불/

A shortening of the well-known phrase, "*Naega hamyeon romance, nami hamyeon bulryun*" (내가 하면 로맨스, 남이 하면 불륜; meaning "If I love someone, it is a romance, but if others do, it is an affair"). This is a sarcastic term used to criticise the double standards of those who take a hypocritical attitude, for example those who consider their affairs true love but those of others infidelity. It has become commonly used across media outlets, from TV and newspaper to magazines, and while sometimes it is mistaken as a Sino-Korean idiomatic expression, only the "*bul*" part is Sino-Korean. <Kyosu Shinmun>, a newspaper representing the opinions of professors in South Korea, picked "*ashitabi*" (我是他非) as the key idiomatic phrase of 2020, which similar to *naelonambul*, means "I am right and the other person is wrong"; in this case because the Korean political landscape is polarised into two camps who are always attacking each other, shifting the blame at every opportunity.[137]

# 82.
# Net-Femi
# /넷페미/

A shortening for feminism or feminist on the Korean Web. The term feminist is defined in the Standard Korean Dictionary as "people who follow or claim gender equality". It is used in a similar way to the English word feminist. Historically, in South Korea, feminism and feminist-led social movements have focused on resistance against the Confucian culture that specifies women's obedience to their husbands. However, this reached a turning point around 2015, when young women who are self-proclaimed feminists on the Internet and social media platforms began to be called "Net-Femi".[138]

While mainstream feminist movements in South Korea tended to focus on enhancing women's position in society by influencing decision makers and legislation processes, "Net-Femi" movements focus more on mobilising demonstrations against misogynistic practice. Several radical feminist online communities including Megalia and social media platforms like Twitter are their main sites of operations, and views have been project increasingly forcefully in relation to movements such as the "Me Too" movement. At the same time, however, attempts to tackle misogynistic practices in more radical or extreme forms have often led to sharp confrontations between men and women in Korean online communities, such as Megalia and WOMAD,[139] sometimes called "gender wars". These communities attack each other through trolling and producing fake news, reinforcing a politics of hatred, which has in turn further strengthened an "us versus them" rhetoric provoking social division based on gender essentialism.

# 83.
# Novel comics
## /노블 코믹스/

Novel comics refer to the *Webtoons* serialised on large portals such as KakaoPage and Naver and based on web novels appearing from the mid-2010s. Typical examples of novel comics include <Moonlight Sculptor> (KakaoPage), <Only I Level Up> (KakaoPage), <The Omnipotent Reader Perspective> (Naver), and <Nanomasin> (Naver). Since both Naver and KakaoPages each has their own *Webtoon* and web fiction platforms, this can be seen as a case of broadening the media mix across their platforms. In the case of Korean *Webtoons*, they are often translated and introduced on overseas platforms targeting global audiences including LINE. Naturally, overseas exports of web novels are also increasing.

# 84.
# Oekwi
## /외퀴/

A term that connotes aversion for foreign fans of K-Pop idols, causing controversy on the Korean Web. As the K-Pop boom increased the number of overseas fans, several entertainment companies and agencies started to secure concert ticket quotas for them, but this has attracted complaints of "discriminating Korean fans" from part of the domestic fandom. At first, the complaints were not targeted at overseas fans themselves; yet, as some of their behaviours transgressed "unwritten rules" or taboos in the Korean fandom, there was an increase in antipathy from certain Korean fans towards them.[140] Transgressing behaviours include: (a) cutting in line at concerts; (b) uploading to the Internet photos of funny facial expressions of idols caught on camera; (c) leaving continuously "Eng sub plz" comments on the idols' social media accounts or live streaming, overshadowing other comments.

# 85.
# Oelangdungi
## /외랑둥이/

A related term to *oekwi* is "*oe-rang-dung-i*", a compound of "*oe-guk-in*" (외국인; foreigner) and "*sa-rang-dung-i*" (사랑둥이; lovelies), thus meaning international lovelies. This term is used to refer to overseas fans in a positive and loving way, and was coined and made known by the BTS's Korean fandom (ARMY) with a view to resolving conflicts and frictions with overseas fans. BTS themselves also apply this term, sometimes calling their fans "*sa-rang-dung-i*" or lovelies.[141]

# 86.
# Pack
## /팩/

A catchall phrase for mask. It is used interchangeably to mean sheet mask or cream, gel or any wash-off masks. However, wash-off varieties are often not referred to by names other than "pack".

# 87.
## Padepri
### /파데프리/

A phrase derived from the Korean transliteration of the term "foundation-free". This refers to a 2020/21 trend following the global pandemic. According to market research agency Kantar, 70% of South Korean women aged 16 to 65 wore significantly less makeup after the pandemic, giving rise to a *padepri* trend.[142]

# 88.
## Paein
### /페인/

A term referring to an avid fan of TV drama. Its etymology comes from the characterisation as a paein someone who binge-watch dramas, to the degree that affects their daily life. In the early 2000s when the Internet was becoming more widely used, niche TV dramas such as <Ruler of Your Own World> (2002) and <Damo> (2003) were watched intensively among viewers in their 20s and 30s[143]; viewers posted about the dramas, referring to themselves as *paein*, and the term has been used widely ever since.

# 89.
# Pinkfong
## /핑크퐁/

An educational content brand created by SmartStudy, a South Korean educational entertainment company. It is the most popular hit ever made by Korean cultural industries, holding various records including the most watched video on YouTube (approximately 8.8 billion views), 49.7 million YouTube subscribers,[144] and No. 1 on Billboard's Emerging Artists Chart.[145]

However, as is the case with most start-ups, the company suffered from financial difficulties in the early days. In 2012, it began expanding the business, starting with purveying a paid *Webtoon* platform service that showed comics by artist Kim Seong-mo, who mainly draws comics for adults.[146] Ever since the <Baby Shark> song sang by Pinkfong characters went viral, however, they have been on the road to success.

# 90.
# Point makeup
## /포인트 메이크업/

A term popular in Korean and Japanese colour cosmetic industry for describing colour makeup for eyes, lips and cheeks. Makeup product lines are referred to using this category split. The categorisation is also widely understood in many parts of East Asia and South East Asia where Korean and Japanese beauty exports dominate.

# 91.
# Ramdon
## /램동/

The food that the young mother of a wealthy family might ask the housekeeper to prepare with premium *Hanwoo* beef, on the way back from a family camping trip. In Korea, it was originally called *Jjapaguri*, as it is essentially the mixing of two instant noodle packages together: *Jjapaghetti* and *Neoguri*. According to the Namuwiki, a Korean wiki built using contributions from netizens, it is believed to have originated in the kitchen division of the South Korean army. In 2013, a reality television show called <Dad! Where Are We Going?> introduced to the mainstream media for the first time the recipe for *Jjapaguri*.[147] Then, in 2020, Bong Joon-ho's <Parasite> (2019) became the first non-English-language film to win an Oscar for best picture, gaining the global spotlight. Thus, *Jjapaguri* attracted further attention. The film critic Darcy Paquet, the English subtitle translator for <Parasite>, cleverly translated *Jjapaguri* as "*Ramdon*", a mash-up of "ramen" and "udon", modifying the word to fit in the English context.[148]

Photo of "*ramdon*" inspired by the film <Parasite>

# 92.
# Ramyun
# /라면/

Instant noodles in Korea are called *ramyun*. While its origin is known to be one kind of Chinese hand-pulled noodle, made by pulling wheat flour dough into long, elastic strips, it is Japanese instant noodle, or ramen (ラーメン), which actually influenced Korean *ramyun*. In Japan, since around the 1870s, noodle soups where pulled noodles are served in a chicken, pork, anchovy, or bonito broth-based soup are called ramen. In 1958, Nissin Foods in Japan invented the contemporary form of instant noodles,[149] which are sold in a precooked (fried) and dried noodle block along with soup powder and dehydrated vegetable stock.

In South Korea, it was in 1963 that Jung-yoon Jeon, the founder of a Korean food company Samyang debuted the first instant noodle under the brand "Samyang *ramyun*". As he witnessed in the post-Korean war period poor people eating "*ggulggul-i juk*" (꿀꿀이죽), a kind of stew made from leftover foods and food waste dumped from the U.S. army, he decided to develop inexpensive and filling foods, and learnt instant noodle-making from Japan. *Ramyun* is a Korean-modified word for ramen.[150]

# 93.
# Sasaeng
## /사생/

A neologism created as a mash-up of "私生" (a Sino-Korean word meaning private life) and "fan". It refers to oversolic-itous fans who track even the private everyday life of their favourite celebrities, especially K-Pop idol bands. In extreme cases, not only do they chase after K-Pop bands 24/7, they also tail the bands" private vehicles, and sometimes even break into their private residences. In 2012, an idol group JYJ (Kim Jae-joong, Park Yoo-cheon, Kim Jun-su) was caught up in rumour that they had assaulted their sasaeng fans, but they then showed how they had long been vic-timised by the fans. According to JYJ, these *sasaeng* fans secretly installed GPS in the members" vehicles to tail them, intruded into their private residence and tried to kiss them, and even crashed into their vehicles just to see their fac-es.[151] Later, as *sasaeng* fans' invasion of privacy has sparked increasing controversy, many argue that they should not be called sasaeng "fans", but simply *sasaeng*, or even stalkers, or criminal.

A related term is "*sasaeng* taxi", which is sometimes shortened as "*sataek*". This is the kind of taxi sasaeng fans use to follow the K-Pop idols. The *sasaeng* taxi drivers make money by picking up and driving *sasaeng* fans around the broadcasting stations or the idol's residences, and tracking their vehicles and transport.[152] The drivers have built up a kind of symbiotic relationship with *sasaeng* fans, and are often complicit in *sasaeng* activities, for example texting *sasaeng* fans to continuously update them on the location of various idols and celebrities.

# 94.
## Seuming
### /스밍/

The Korean abbreviated pronunciation of the English word "streaming". It refers to such fandom activities as continuously streaming their favourite idols' newly-released songs and music videos across multiple social media and music streaming platforms, with a view to supporting them. As a result of seuming, these songs and videos gain increased views and recommendations, and so will more likely enter the top of the charts.

# 95.
# 7 Skin
## /7 스킨/

The 7 Skin Method is a popular home skin treatment method. It is done by applying up to seven layers of hydrators, toners or essences to achieve hydrated and glowing skin. Although seven is the number of layers in the method's namesake, users adjust the number of layers according to how hydrated their skin feels after each layer.

Fans of the method often report benefits such as less visible pores, radiant skin and skin texture, and less sebaceous skin.[153] However, some dermatologists doubt the efficacy of this method, especially when carried out on sensitive and dry skin and as a replacement for a proper moisturising regime.[154] There are also concerns that this method exposes the skin to sensitising levels of ingredients such as exfoliants (acids), fragrance, essential oils, alcohol and other astringents.

# How to practice the 7 Skin Method effectively?

\*

1. Choose toners without exfoliants, menthol, fragrance, essential oils, alcohol or have astringent qualities. This includes witch hazel!

2. Choose toners that contain moisture attracting ingredients.

3. Use light and watery toners for oilier skins.

4. Moisturise as usual after your last step. No amount of toner can substitute the function of a moisturiser.

# 96.
# Sleeping pack
## /수면팩/

The sleeping pack is a derivative of pack (see entry 86). It is usually a gel, gel-cream or lotion format mask that is meant to be layered onto skin and left on overnight. It is usually formulated to absorb into skin or evaporate over the course of the night. The concept is centred around delivering a dose of hydration and skin treatment during sleep hours to take advantage of the body's natural recovery cycle.

# 97.
# Soju
# /소주/

A clear, colourless distilled alcoholic beverage, the most popular alcoholic beverage in Korea. While it is the second most-consumed beverage (after beer), due to its relatively high alcohol content, it is the most frequently drunk, and is a drink truly loved by Koreans.[155]

Etymologically, *soju* means "burnt liqueur", with the first syllable "*so*" referring to the heat of distillation. It originated in the 13th Century Goryeo Dynasty, when Levantine distillation techniques were introduced from Arabia to the Yuan Mongols, and then to Korea, when Genghis Khan's grandson Kublai Khan advanced into the Korean peninsula during the times of King Chungnyeol, in an attempt to invade Japan.[156]

Traditionally, *soju* referred to the alcoholic beverage made by distilling *takju* (*makgeolli*), *yakju*, or *cheongju*. Like cognac or whisky, *soju* was traditionally made using the pot still method, and a large amount of rice was turned into a small amount of alcohol; hence, the expensive price. However, since the continuous distillation method invented in the West in the early 20th Century was introduced via Japan,[157] and the South Korean government prohibited the traditional distillation of *soju* from rice, many *soju* makers started making it the "diluted" way. In this manner, *soju* is created by "diluting" highly distilled ethanol made via the continuous distillation of sweet potatoes or tapioca, mixing it with flavourings, sweeteners and water.[158] Due to its easy mass production, diluted *soju* soon came to take precedence over traditional distilled *soju* in Korean society, and most of the *sojus* that are currently sold at Korean supermarkets are of this kind. Most diluted *sojus* are transparent, with an alcohol level varying from 16.9% ("Good Day") to 20.1% ("*Chamisul* Classic"). While several artisan *sojus* are still made using traditional distillation techniques ("*Andong soju*" and "*Hwayo*", for example) and enjoy popularity among *soju* aficionados, they are comparatively expensive.[159]

# 98.
# Somaek
## /소맥/

*Somaek* is cocktail made by mixing *soju* and beer to a certain ratio. The name is a syllabic abbreviation of *soju* and *maekju* (beer). *Soju* has a high alcohol content, so drinking a large amount can be difficult, while beer's fizziness may not be appealing to all drinkers. Therefore, some prefer a mixture of the two, offering a relatively moderate alcohol volume, with a softer texture. Yet, there are differing opinions as to the ideal ratio between *soju* and beer, sometimes referred to as the "golden ratio". According to a survey by the HiteJinro, a distiller in South Korea, the most popular ratio was 40:127 *soju*:beer.[160] Indeed, several of the blogs on the Korean Web recommend a similar ratio of 1:3.

"*Soju*" is generally preferred in South Korean drinking culture, and particularly when eating Korean BBQ or *samgyeopsal* (sliced and grilled pork belly). South Koreans also make "*somaek*", a mixture of *soju* and beer, to heighten the buzz and excitement.

# 99.
# V-app
## /브이앱/

A platform where idols live stream. The official name is "V Live", but it is commonly called V-app on the Korean Web. Naver Corporation launched the service on the 1st of September 2015. As its launching promotional slogan "connect K-Pop stars with overseas fans" suggests,[161] unlike many other user-generated platforms where any users can freely participate and broadcast, V-app only approves of the channels associated with K-Pop stars, and only allows these celebrities to live stream. On January 27, 2021, it was announced that, in a strategic alliance, V Live service will be merged with the Weverse platform operated by Hybe Corporation (formerly Big Hit Entertainment, managers of BTS).[162]

Here, Weverse is an online platform and mobile app that hosts K-Pop-artist-to-fan communication channels for direct and diverse interactions, and sells subscriptions for multimedia content, band-related products and merchandise. It is available in English for users from across the world, and will launch live streaming from 2022.

# 100.
# Webtoon
## /웹툰/

*Webtoon* is a term used to describe South Korean Webcomics or *manhwa* published via online media platforms. With the penetration of high-speed Internet towards the end of the 1990s, *Webtoons* became known through personal websites or blogs of amateur cartoonists.[163] This was possible due to web and digital technologies lowering the cost of digital image creation by reducing the need for drawing tools (e.g. drawing pens, screentone), while enhancing the readiness with which larger audiences could be reached.

Since the mid-2000s, web portals have further expanded these opportunities, providing "free" online platforms committed to the publication of *Webtoons*, eliminating creators' need to pay hosting fees for multiple individual websites, and offering more extensive opportunities to interact with myriad users on the web portals.[164]

In production terms, *Webtoon* generally comprise vertically arranged images, which users scroll from top to bottom. This mode of presentation allows content creators to show one large-size image on screen, making it less restricted in terms of the "layout" of images, something which is crucial for storytelling in printed comic strips[165] and other web/digital comics that observe the same type of image arrangement.[166]

With the domestic *Webtoon* market already valued

at US $368 million by the mid-2010s,[167] *Webtoon* platforms started global services to encompass wider digital comics markets. Naver now provides global services under different names, including "LINE *Manga*" in Japanese, "*Dongman Manhua*" and *Webtoon* in Chinese, and simply *Webtoon* in English, French, Indonesian, Spanish, Thai and German.

In the pandemic era, where cultural consumption has been encouraged through the rise of contactless inter-actions, global consumption of *Webtoons* has seen a further increase. According to Naver, the number of monthly active users worldwide in March 2020 exceeded 62 million, up sharply from 60 million the previous year.[168]

# Endnotes

1        Lee, S. (2012). Hallyu in Europe as a phenomenon of cultural hybridization-with the analysis on K-pop Craze [유럽의 '한류'를 통해 본 문화혼종화: K-pop 열풍을 중심으로]. *Koreanisch-Deutsche Gesellschaft für Sozialwissenschaften*, 22, pp.117-146. See also KOCIS (2012). *Korean Wave: From K-Pop to K-Culture* [한류: K-Pop에서 K-Culture로]. KOCIS (Korean Culture and Information Service).

2        KOFICE (2019). *A Study on the Impact of the Korean Wave in 2018* [2018 한류 파급효과 연구]. KOFICE (Korean Culture and Information Service).

3        KIET (2015). *Policy measures to strengthen the competitiveness of K-Pop* [K-Pop의 경쟁력 강화를 위한 정책방안]. KIET (Korean Institute for Industrial Economics & Trade). See also Lee, S. (2012).

4        Shizuka, H. (2018). Gender Identities and Ideologies in Korean Students' Talk: Focusing on the meta discourses regarding 'aegyo' [한국 대학생들의 말하기를 통해서 보는 젠더 아이덴티티와 젠더 이데올로기: '애교'에 대한 메타담론을 중심으로]. 비교문화연구, 24(2), pp.431-470.

5        Naik, M. (2016). Hills and valleys: Understanding the under-eye. *Journal of Cutaneous and Aesthetic Surgery*, 9(2), p.61. See also Dr. Siew, T.W. (2013). 'Aegyo-Sal : Eye-Bags for a Youthful Appearance?', *Dr Siew.com* [online]. Available at: https://drsiew.com/aegyo-sal-eye-bags-for-a-youthful-appearance

6        Lacey, M.D. (2013). 'Why are Korean women having surgery to make their under-eye bags BIGGER?', *Daily Mail*, 26

Jul [online]. Available at: https://www.dailymail.co.uk/femail/article-2378854/Bigger-eye-bags-New-Korean-trend-puffy-eyes-aegyo-sal-make-surgery-filler-fat-grafts.html

7        Cho, C. (2021). 'Charlotte Cho Shares How to Perfect The Aegyo-Sal Look: The Klog', *Soko Gram*, 2 Feb[online]. Available at: https://sokoglam.com/blogs/news/10924529-the-tutorial-aegyo-sal

8        Afreeca TV (2014). 'Introduction to Afreeca TV Service', *Afreeca TV* [online]. Available at: http://www.afreecatv.com/cooperation/Afreeca_Introduction.pdf

9        Ryu, S. and S. Lee (2013). Development Direction of Video Contents Service in Mobile Era: on the Case of Afreeca-TV [모바일 시대의 영상 콘텐츠 서비스 발전 방향- 아프리카 TV 사례를 중심으로]. *Korea Contents Institution*, 2013(5), pp.155-156.

10        Lee, D., S. Lee and Hong, N. (2016). Smart media era Internet private broadcasting regulation system improvement [스마트 미디어 시대 인터넷 개인 방송 규제 체계 정비]. *South Korea National Assembly Research Service*, p.10.

11        Jin, D. (2010). *Korea's Online Gaming Empire*. Cambridge, Mass.: MIT Press.

12        Afreeca TV (2014).

13        Kim, H. (2015). A Study on Food Porn as a Sub-Culture - Centering on Internet "Meokbang" (eating scene) in Afreeca TV [하위문화로서의 푸드 포르노(Food Porn) 연구: 아프리카TV의 인터넷 먹방을 중심으로]. 인문학연구, 50, p. 437.

14      Park, H. (2019), '[신조어 사전] 어그로', *Seoul Daily*, 6 Oct [Online]. Available at: https://www.sedaily.com/News-VIew/1VPF2D91SP

15      Park, S. (2019). '악플 정글에 방치된 웹툰... "연재를 중단합니다"', *Hankook Ilbo*, 30 Nov [Online]. Available at: https://www.hankookilbo.com/News/Read/201911220085016129

16      Ibid.

17      DJUNA (2016). '<아수라>, 또 하나의 '알탕 영화'', *Hankyoreh*, 10 Oct [Online]. Available at: https://www.hani.co.kr/arti/culture/movie/764880.html

18      Gang, P. (2017). '천만 영화에 여성은 없다', *Women News*, 29 Nov [Online]. Available at: https://www.womennews.co.kr/news/articleView.html?idxno=128326

19      Kim, S. (2019). '통계로 재확인된 영화계 남초 현상', *Nocut News*, 7 Oct [Online]. Available at: https://www.nocutnews.co.kr/news/5224359.

20      Ibid.

21      Kim, B., E. Choi, Nam, D., W. Kim, Jung, H., and A. Bechdel (2019). *House of Hummingbird* [벌새]. Arte.

22      Kim, Y. (2020). '10 Korean films make 'Bechdel Choice 10' list for promoting gender equality', *Korea JoongAng Daily,* 12 Aug [Online]. Available at: https://koreajoongangdaily.joins.com/2020/08/12/entertainment/movies/Directors-Guild-of-Korea-Bechdel-Choice-10-Bechdel-test/20200812174000375.html

23      Bell-Young, L. (2021). 'The Evolution of The Ampoule', *ReAgent*, 10 Feb[online]. Available at: https://www.reagent.co.uk/the-evolution-of-the-ampoule

24      Sung, M. (2019). '에센스, 세럼, 앰플…얼마나 다를까, *Newsis*, 25 Apr [Online]. Available at: https://newsis.com/view/?id=NISX20190424_0000631354

25      Ibid.

26      Cho, K. (2017). 'Baedal (倍達)' [배달], *Encyclopedia of Korean culture* [Online]. Available at: http://encykorea.aks.ac.kr/Contents/Item/E0021854

27      Chung, G. (2015). 'How South Korea's AmorePacific Became One Of The World's Most Innovative Companies', *Forbes*, 19 Aug [online]. Available at: https://www.forbes.com/sites/gracechung/2015/08/19/how-south-koreas-amorepacific-became-one-of-the-worlds-most-innovative-companies

28      Latimer, J. (2012). 'BB cream fans lay it on thick', *Macleans*, 11 Jan [Online]. Available at: https://www.macleans.ca/economy/business/bb-cream-fans-lay-it-on-thick/

29      Dr med Christine Schrammek UK (n.d.). 'Dr Schrammek', *Dr Schrammek* [online]. Available at: https://drschrammek.co.uk

30      Lee, Y. (2016). '아, 내 댓글이 무심히 파묻혔다 TT', *Hankyoreh*, 25 Sep [Online]. Available at: https://www.hani.co.kr/arti/culture/culture_general/762660.html

31      Official website. Available at: https://comic.naver.com/genre/bestChallenge.nhn

32      Chin, S. (2012). The culturality which is inherent in Korean traditional foods: In Relationship with the Globalization Strategy [한국전통음식에 내재한 문화성: 세계화 전략과 관련하여]. *Journal of Next-generation Convergence Information Services*, 1(1), pp. 41-56.

33      Jun, Y. (2011). A Study on Traditional Beauty of Korean Bojagi: Focused On The Bojagi and Patchwork Wrapping Cloth of The Joseon Dynasty [한국 보자기의 전통미에 관한 고찰: 조선중기 보자기와 조각보를 중심으로]. *Art Education Review*, 39, pp. 211-242.

34      Hermes (n.d.). 'L'Art du Bojagi shawl 140', *Hermes* [Online]. Available at: https://www.hermes.cn/cn/en/product/l-art-du-bojagi-shawl-140-H243205Sv16/

35      Waddoups, R. (2019). 'Designer of the Day: Adam Pogue', *Surface*, 29 Oct [Online]. Available at: https://www.surface-mag.com/articles/adam-pogue-designer-day/

36      Han, G. (2017). '브로맨스와 위맨스', *Women Times*, 27 Jul [Online]. Available at: https://www.womentimes.co.kr/news/articleView.html?idxno=37961

37      Kim, D. (2021). '뜨거운 맛과 깊은 맛, 新브로맨스로 풍성해진 안방극장', *Weekly Hankooki*, 22 Mar [Online]. Available at: https://weekly.hankooki.com/lpage/entv/202103/wk20210322130847146690.htm

38      Hwang, J. (2016). '방탄소년단 "방시혁이 탄생시킨 소년단? 편견 막아내겠다는 뜻"', *Donga Ilbo*, 12 May [Online]. Available at: https://www.donga.com/news/Entertainment/article/all/20160512/78059011/1

39      Shin, Y. (2020). '방탄소년단 '다이너마이트' 발표…코로나19 극복 위로하는 문화의 힘', *The Kyeong-gi Shinmun*, 22 Aug [Online]. Available at: https://kgnews.co.kr/mobile/article.html?no=599316

40      Kim, J. (2018). 'How BTS Are Breaking K-Pop's Biggest Taboos', *RollingStone*, 29 May [Online]. Available at: https://www.rollingstone.com/music/music-news/how-bts-are-breaking-k-pops-biggest-taboos-628141/

41      Kim, J., M. Shin, and Do, J. (2020). *Bumping into BTS*. Jikim Publishing Limited.

42      Burns, C.T. (2021). 'The 15 CC Creams That Do Way More Than Color Correct', *Byrdie*, 5 May [online]. Available at: https://www.byrdie.com/best-cc-creams-4707579

43      Cho, G. (2005). '길들일 수 없는 괴물의 탄생', *Han-kyoreh 21*, 2 Feb [Online]. Available at: http://h21.hani.co.kr/arti/PRINT/13127.html

44      Lee, H. (2006). Watching the masculinity of Korean Broadcasting Dramas [한국방송드라마의 남성성보기]. 문학과영상학회 학술대회 발표논문집, pp.13–22.

45      Park, E. (2014). Structure of Story and Characteristics of Protagonists in Television Melodramas: Focusing on Three Major Broadcasters [텔레비전 멜로드라마의 이야기구조와 남녀주인공의 특성: 방송 3사를 중심으로]. *The Journal of the Korea Contents Association*, 14(2), pp.48–59.

46      Shing, W. (2009). The problem of Cinderella Complex review in the Korea drama :Focus Korea-style [한국 드라마를 통

해 본 '신데렐라 콤플렉스' 비평의 문제점 – <꽃보다 남자>를 중심으로]. 한민족문화연구, 31, pp.493–524.

47      Wow TV (2021). '총공, 스밍... 아이돌 덕질 용어 무슨 뜻이야?', *WowTV*, 24 Feb [online]. Available at: https://www.wowtv.co.kr/NewsCenter/News/Read?articleId=A201602230607

48      American Academy of Dermatology Association (n.d.). 'Scars: Signs and symptoms', *AAD* [online]. Available at: https://www.aad.org/public/diseases/a-z/scars-symptoms.

49      Jang, J. (2018). 'Why K-beauty is crazy about cica creams', *Mintel* [online]. Available at: https://www.mintel.com/blog/beauty-market-news/why-k-beauty-is-crazy-about-cica-creams-1

50      Ratz-lyko, A., J. Arct, and Pytkowska, K. (2016). Moisturizing and anti-inflammatory properties of cosmetic formulations containing Centella asiatica extract. *Indian Journal of Pharmaceutical Sciences*, 78(1), p.27.

51      Gohil, K., Patel, J. and Gajjar, A. (2010). Pharmacological review on Centella asiatica: A potential herbal cure-all. *Indian Journal of Pharmaceutical Sciences*, 72(5), p.546.

52      Naver (2020). '클린봇 2.0: 문맥을 이해하는 악성 댓글(단문) 탐지 AI', *Naver*, 16 Jul [Online]. Available at: https://d2.naver.com/helloworld/7753273

53      Han, S. (2021). '네이버웹툰이 온통 '쿠키'로 도배된 사연', *Hankook Ilbo*, 1 Apr [Online]. Available at: https://www.hankookilbo.com/News/Read/A2021040115400003301

54      Kim, G. and Seo, J. (2014). 'Global luxury cosmetics brands copy AmorePacific's cushion cosmetics', *Pulse*, 3 Dec [online]. Available at: https://pulsenews.co.kr/view.php?year=2014&no=1490749 [Accessed 23 May 2021].

55      Park, J. (2018). 'Korea's supremacy in cushion compact at stake', *The Korea Times*, 12 Jun [online]. Available at: https://www.koreatimes.co.kr/www/tech/2020/07/129_250531.html [Accessed 23 May 2021].

56      Abrenica, S. (2020). '12 Cushion Compacts for Smooth, Seamless Skin', *Byrdie*, 11 Nov. [online] Available at: https://www.byrdie.com/best-cushion-compacts-4159716 [Accessed 23 May 2021].

57      Lee, B (2020). '달고나 커피, 저을수록 찐득해지는 이유는?', *Donga Science*, May [Online]. Available at: https://dl.dongascience.com/magazine/

58      BBC (n.d.). 'Dalgona coffee', *BBC Food* [Online]. Available at: https://www.bbc.co.uk/food/recipes/dalonga_coffee_20606

59      Lee, J. (2016). '고대뉴스 취미를 직업으로, 덕업일치 이뤄낸 성공한 덕후들', *KU News*, 29 May [Online]. Available at: http://www.kunews.ac.kr/news/articlePrint.html?idxno=22978

60      Lee, A (2019). ''일코? 덕밍아웃? '그녀의 사생활' 덕후 용어 사전 공개', *JoongAng Ilbo*, 5 Apr [Online]. Available at: https://news.joins.com/article/23432580

61      Yu, S (2020). '''취집' 꿈꾸는 여성총리?…힘 못쓰는 로코·멜로 시대 [출처: 중앙일보] '취집' 꿈꾸는 여성총리?…힘 못쓰는 로코·멜로 시대', *JoongAng Ilbo*, 5 May [Online]. Available at: https://news.joins.com/article/23769158

62      Kim, H. (2013). Discovering and Representing 'Dong-in-nyo' in Korea: Focusing on Examples from Korean Girls' Comic ['동인녀(同人女)'의 발견과 재현: 한국 순정만화의 사례를 중심으로]. 아시아문화연구, 30, pp.43-75.

63      Lezhin, https://www.lezhin.com/ko/comic/dooly

64      Line Friends, https://www.linefriends.com/?lang=ko

65      Kim, I. (2019). '검증된 작가·'가족' 소재의 힘… KBS2 주말극 '20년째 불패신화', *Munhwa Ilbo*, 19 Feb [Online]. Available at: http://www.munhwa.com/news/view.html?no=2019021901032439179001

66      Yun, S. (2019). A Study on the Aspects of Family Liberalization in Korean Television Family Drama- Focusing on KBS2 TV Weekend Soap Operas [한국 텔레비전 가족드라마의 가족자유주의 양상: KBS2 TV 주말연속극을 대상으로]. 어문논총, 34, pp.37-79.

67      IICNET (1999). *A Study on the Development of Korea traditional food's Web site* [한국전통음식 웹사이트 개발에 관한 연구]. IICNET, p.41.
See also Encyclopedia of Korean Culture, http://encykorea.aks.ac.kr/Contents/Item/E0004012

68      Jung, K. (2019). The History of Sunchang Gochujang [순창고추장의 역사]. 한국콘텐츠학회 춘계종합학술대회, 17 May, pp.215-216.

69      Lee, S. (2018). '온라인 '고나리' 화제 왜? 의미 뭐길래?', *The Kookje Daily News*, 17 Jul [Online]. Available at: http://www.kookje.co.kr/news2011/asp/newsbody.asp?code=0300&key=20180717.99099008137

70      See KBS (2018). '"수능보다 어렵다"는 공카고시의 실체', *KBS*, 26 Sep [Online]. Available at: https://news.kbs.co.kr/news/view.do?ncd=4042746

71      Mize, D. (2008). 'Gradation: A Powerful Technique for Unifying Paintings', *Empty Easel*, 9 Sep [Online]. Available at: https://emptyeasel.com/2008/09/09/gradation-a-powerful-technique-for-unifying-paintings/ [Accessed 23 May 2021].

72      Martin, J. (1992). *The encyclopedia of pastel techniques.* Philadelphia, Penn.: Running Press.

73      Jung, H. (2020). '해외가 '깜짝' 놀랐다고? 지나친 유튜브 '국뽕' 콘텐트, 근원은', *Joongang Ilbo*, 4 Sep [Online]. Available at: https://news.joins.com/article/23864922

74      KOCIS (2012). *Korean Wave: From K-Pop to K-Culture* [한류: K-Pop에서 K-Culture로]. KOCIS (Korean Culture and Information Service).

75      Lee C. (2016) 'Why more Koreans are eating alone', *Korea Herald*, 24 May [online]. Available at: http://www.koreaherald.com/view.php?ud=20160529000252

76      Ibid.

77      Go, M. (2014). '커핀그루나루, 허니버터칩과 허니버터 브랜드의 평행이론', *Money Today*, 24 Dec [Online]. Available at: https://news.mt.co.kr/mtview.php?no=2014122322411038445

78      An, H. (2019). '길림양행, 만수르 왕자도 찾는 '허니버터 아몬드' 만들다', *Korea Economic Daily*, 7 Jul [Online]. Available at: https://www.hankyung.com/economy/article/2019070769341

79      Seo, Y. (2016). '식품업계 점령한 '단짠' 열풍⋯국민 건강은 뒷전?', *Daily Consumer News Channel*, 23 Aug [Online]. Available at: http://www.dailycnc.com/news/articleView.html?idxno=58903

80      Lee, H. (2020). '불닭볶음면으로 'K푸드' 선도', *Woman Donga*, 21 Sep [Online]. Available at: https://woman.donga.com/3/all/12/2188346/1

81      Ibid.

82      Kim, S. (2011). A Study on the Masculinity Image of Male Idol Stars and the Construction of Fandom Identity: Focusing on 2PM and SHINee [남성 아이돌 스타의 남성성 재현과 성인 여성 팬덤의 소비 방식 구성]. *Media, Gender and Culture*, 19, pp.5-38.

83      Kim, Y. (2019). 'K팝이라는 모순: 아이돌 음악과 다양성에 대한 고찰', *Hallyu Now*, Apr [Online]. Available at: http://kofice.or.kr/b20industry/b20_industry_03_view.asp?seq=7988

84      Kim, S. (2011).

85      Lee, J. and S. Seo (2017). A Study on the Characteristics of Female Idol Star's Fashion Image Depending on the Different Type of Fandom [팬덤 층 유형에 따른 여성아이돌 패션 이미지 특성]. *Journal of the Korean Society of Costume*, 67(8), pp.1-19.

86      Ilbe, www.ilbe.com

87      Kim, J. (2018). Misogyny for male solidarity: Online hate discourse against women in South Korea. In *Mediating Misogyny* (pp.151-169). Palgrave Macmillan.

88      See examples at https://comic.naver.com/webtoon/genre.nhn?genre=daily

89      See Encyclopedia of Korean Culture, http://encykorea.aks.ac.kr/Contents/SearchNavi?keyword=%EC%9D%B8%EC%82%BC%C&ridx=0&tot=86

90      Ibid.

91      Jung, J. (2011). '귀여니 교수 임용 논란 국어파괴자가 교수를?', JoongAng Ilbo, 5 Jul [Online]. Available at: https://news.joins.com/article/5740044

92      Ryu, J. (2018). '<늑대의 유혹> 어떤 작품이기에', Sisun News, 22 Oct [Online]. Avaialble at: https://www.sisunnews.co.kr/news/articleView.html?idxno=91937

93      See examples at http://www.joara.com/main.html

94      Shin, H. (2016). K-pop, the sound of subaltern cosmopolitanism? In Routledge Handbook of East Asian Popular Culture (pp.130-137). Routledge.

95      YTN (2018). '팬심의 진화, 조공 문화의 모든 것', YTN, 28 Jun [Online]. Available at: https://www.ytn.co.kr/_ln/0102_201806281632125857

96      Cho, W. and J. Tae (2018). A Study on the Sociocultural Implications of 'Gift Culture' ['조공문화'에 대한 사회문화적 함의 연구]. 글로벌문화콘텐츠학회 학술대회자료집, 2018, pp.219-223.

97      Han, S. (2021). '그룹 여자친구, "손편지 제외한 팬 서포트 안받는다"…조공 거절한 아이돌 누구?', TopStar News, 13 Jan [Online]. Available at: http://www.topstarnews.net/news/articleV-

iew.html?idxno=855793

98      Kim, J. (2019). '"내 팬은 내가 챙긴다" 아이돌 스타들의 '역조공'을 아시나요', *Donga Ilbo*, 27 Nov [Online]. Available at: https://www.donga.com/news/Culture/article/all/20191127/98550262/1

99      An, Y. (2009). '미디어법 탄생부터 처리까지', *Yonhap News Agency*, 22 Jul [Online]. Available at: https://www.yna.co.kr/view/AKR20090722178600001

100     Kim, K. (2002). *The Fantasy of Korean Blockbuster, Narcissism of Korean Film* [한국 블록버스터의 환상, 한국영화의 나르시시즘]. Chaeksesang.
See also Cho, S. (2004). Family Romance and Collective Unconsciousness Represented in Korean Gangster Movies[한국 조폭 영화에 내재된 가족 로망스와 현대 한국인의 집단 무의식]. *The Journal of Literature and Film*, 5(1), pp.103-125.

101     See Rotten Tomatoes, https://www.rottentomatoes.com/tv/kingdom_2019

102     Nam, J. (2021). '"역사 왜곡' 논란에…SBS, '조선구마사' 결국 방영 취소', *Hankyoreh*, 26 Mar [Online]. Available at: https://www.hani.co.kr/arti/culture/culture_general/988344.html

103     Lee, S. (2012). Hallyu in Europe as a Phenomenon of Cultural Hybridization: with the analysis on K-pop Craze [유럽의 '한류'를 통해 본 문화혼종화: K-pop 열풍을 중심으로]. *ZdKDGS*, 22(1), pp.117-146.

104     KIET (2015). *Policy measures to strengthen the competitiveness of K-Pop* [K-Pop의 경쟁력 강화를 위한 정책방안]. KIET (Korean Institute for Industrial Economics & Trade).

See also Lee, S. (2012), p.274.

105    Kraidy, M.(2006). *Hybridity, or the cultural logic of globalization*. Temple University Press.

106    Kim, B. (2014a). '2014 대한민국 밤의 식탁문화', *Donga Ilbo*, 23 Sep [online]. Available at: http://news.donga.com/List/Series_70030000000712/3/7003 0000000712/20140920/66542963/1

107    Son, D. (2017) '시장 규모 3조원 한국 대표 야식 '치킨'··· 닭고기 소비량 미국의 1/3, 성장 잠재력 커', *Chosun Ilbo*, 20 Feb [online]. Available at: http://premium.chosun.com/site/data/html_dir/2017/02/01/2017020101184.html

108    Sang, Y. (2015) 'Korean fried chicken places outnumber world's McDonald's', *Korea herald*, 5 Oct [online]. Available at: http://www.koreaherald.com/view.php?ud=20151005001042

109    Fortune (2016). 'South Korea's Fried Chicken Craze Sparks Battle for Market Share', *Fortune*, 17 Oct [online]. Available at: https://fortune.com/2016/10/17/korea-fried-chicken-%20production/

110    Rural Development Administration (2011). *Kimchi, Taste of Thousand Years* [천년의 맛, 김치를 말하다]. RDA [Online]. Available at: https://www.korea.kr/archive/expDocView.do?docId=30057

111    Park, C. (2019). Comprehensive Study on the Origins and Changes in Kimchi Recipe [김치의 기원과 제조변천과정에 대한 종합적 연구]. *Journal of the Korean Society of Food Culture*, 34(2), pp.93-111.

112      Republic of Korea (2013). 'Kimjang, making and sharing kimchi in the Republic of Korea' Inscribed in 2013 on *the Representative List of the Intangible Cultural Heritage of Humanity*. UNESCO [Online]. Available at: https://ich.unesco.org/en/RL/kimjang-making-and-sharing-kimchi-in-the-republic-of-korea-00881

113      Lee, Y. (2000). The implications of approval of international food standards for Kimchi [김치의 국제식품규격 승인의 의미]. *Bulletin of Food Technology*, 13(3), pp.64-49.

114      Raymond, J. (2013). 'World's Healthiest Foods: Kimchi (Korea)', *Health*, 26 Jun [Online]. Available at: https://www.health.com/condition/digestive-health/worlds-healthiest-foods-kimchi-korea

115      Kim, B. (2020). '코로나에 효과 논문까지...글로벌 시장 김치 러브콜', *Seoul Economic Daily*, 28 Sep [Online]. Available at: https://www.sedaily.com/NewsVIew/1Z80PBNBWA

116      Kim, T. (2020). '태사자 김형준이 '손가락 하트' 원조로 지목됐다', *Huffington Post*, 3 Jan [Online]. Available at: https://www.huffingtonpost.kr/entry/k-finger-heart_kr_5e0ea505e4b0b2520d1f4f46

117      Hur, S. (2009). Pilgrimage to our Traditional Alcohol [우리 전통 술의 순례: 탁주 또는 막걸리 이야기]. *Food culture*, 2(3), pp.114–118.

118      Ibid.

119      Jangsu makgeolli, http://www.koreawine.co.kr/2011/index.php

120     Saengtag makgeolli, http://www.ricewinekorea.co.kr/kor/html/main/main.php

121     Ildong makgeolli, http://xn--369ay3l35ejd457e5hhnxn.kr/niabbs5/

122     Kim, D. (2021). ''올드함' 벗고 '회춘'한 막걸리, 제2의 전성기 오나', *Newsis*, 14 Apr [Online]. Available at: https://newsis.com/view/?id=NISX20210413_0001405275

123     See Standard Korean Language Dictionary, https://stdict.korean.go.kr/main/main.do

124     See <Sky Castle>, https://tv.jtbc.joins.com/skycastle

125     Yu, J. (2013). 'The Foundation Myth: Dangun Story', *Chosun Ilbo for kids*, 26 Sep [Online]. Available at: http://kid.chosun.com/site/data/html_dir/2013/09/25/2013092502633.html

126     Jin, S. (2012). The culturality which is inherent in Korean traditional foods. -In Relationship with the Globalization [한국전통음식에 내재한 문화성]. *Journal of Next-generation Convergence Information Services Technology*, 1(1), pp.41-56.

127     Byun, H. (2021). '세계인 식탁 위에 한국 간편식·가공식품… '한식=불고기' 공식 깼다', *Chosun Ilbo*, 30 Mar [Online]. Available at: https://www.chosun.com/economy/market_trend/2021/03/30/MFUHGS2JIBFVFEDYGL3XLNYCLY/

128     Lee, H. (2020). '비비고 만두 1조 매출…미국서 더 잘 팔린다', *Maeil Business Newspaper*, 18 Oct [Online]. Available at: https://www.mk.co.kr/news/business/view/2020/10/1065698/

129     See Encyclopedia of Korean culture [Online]. Avail-

able at: http://encykorea.aks.ac.kr/Contents/Index?contents_
id=E0019896

130    Cho, J. (2021). '"What is 'MINARI'?"···<미나리> 정
이삭 감독이 밝힌 타이틀의 의미', *Chosun Ilbo*, 26 Jan [Online].
Available at: https://www.chosun.com/entertainments/enter-
tain_photo/2021/01/26/SMOXTPR4A743FGQYD2UPUM6A2I/

131    Farhi, P. (2020). ''Parasite' makes Oscars history as the
first foreign-language film to win best picture', *Washington Post*,
10 Feb [Online]. Available at: https://www.washingtonpost.com/
lifestyle/style/parasite-makes-oscars-history-as-the-first-foreign-
language-film-to-win-best-picture/2020/02/10/93b7e5f8-49fa-
11ea-9164-d3154ad8a5cd_story.html

132    Jung, K. (2010). '언년이 '민폐 리스트'의 모든 것', *JoongAng Ilbo*, 26 May [Online]. Available at: https://news.joins.com/
article/4021472

133    Kim, M. (2017). '김아중 "30대되니 일욕심 많
아져..여배우 위한 작품 부족"', *Start News*, 14 Oct [On-
line]. Available at: https://m.star.mt.co.kr/view.htm-
l?no=2017101313264807075&MS2&ref=

134    Thelwell, E. (2017). 'The next Harry Potter words to
join the dictionary?', *BBC*, 13 Apr [Online]. Available at: https://
www.bbc.co.uk/news/uk-39586989

135    Kim, M. (2018). '입덕을 부르는 '영업왕', '머글킹' 남자
아이돌 7', *Spobiz*, 2 Jul [Online]. Available at: http://www.sporbiz.
co.kr/news/articleView.html?idxno=250986

136    Kim, H. (2015).

137    Lee, E. (2020). '올해의 사자성어는 '아시타비'… '내로남불' 뜻하는 신조어', *ChosunBiz*, 20 Dec [Online]. Available at: https://biz.chosun.com/site/data/html_dir/2020/12/20/2020122000227.html

138    Byun, J. (2016). ''넷 페미' '히포시'가 무슨 뜻?...한글날', *Women News*, 12 Oct [Online]. Available at: http://www.women-news.co.kr/news/articleView.html?idxno=98423

139    Kim, J. (2018).
See also Cho, J. (2019). How Will the World of Freedom for Everyone Approach Us?: Womad's Political Strategies and Young Women as Subjects [모두가 자유로운 세상은 어떻게 우리에게 다가올까?: '워마드'의 정치전략과 젊은 여성주체들]. *Feminism Studies*, 19(2), pp.147-160

140    Kim, J. (2019). ''외퀴' '화이트워싱'…K팝, '인종주의' 덫을 놓았나 덫에 걸렸나', *Kyunghyang Shinmun*, 4 Mar [Online]. Available at: http://news.khan.co.kr/kh_news/khan_art_view.html?art_id=201903041746001

141    Ibid.

142    Monod, O. (2021). 'Top Korean Beauty Trends For 2021 | 뷰티 아트디렉터가 추천하는 2021년 대표 제품은? 추천템 TOP 4', *Youtube* [Online]. Available at: https://www.youtube.com/watch?v=kYNUKPkxfFc [Accessed 23 May 2021].

143    Pi, S. (2003). ''페인'의 힘을 아는가', *Hankyoreh21*, 17 Sep [Online]. Available at: http://h21.hani.co.kr/arti/culture/culture_general/8987.html

144    Park, A. (2021). 'Pinkfong 'Baby Shark Dance' expected to grab YouTube's Ruby Button', *The Korean Times*, 24 Jun

[Online]. Available at: https://m.koreatimes.co.kr/pages/310939.html?gosh

145      Zellner, X. (2019). 'Pinkfong Hits No. 1 on Emerging Artists Chart', *Billboard*, 17 Mar [Online]. Available at: https://www.billboard.com/articles/columns/chart-beat/8504373/pinkfong-no-1-emerging-artists-chart

146      Park, S. (2020.) '해외 매출 80%, 영업이익률 30% … 스마트스터디 10년의 기록, K콘텐츠 신기록 작성은 '진행형'', *Maeil Business Newspaper*, 11 Jun [Online]. Available at: https://www.mk.co.kr/news/business/view/2020/06/599895/

147      Lee, E. (2020). '[D스토리] 짜파구리 생명력 10년, 계획이 다 있었나?', *Yonhap News Agency*, 23 Feb [Online]. Available at:https://www.yna.co.kr/view/AKR20200221138900797

148      Kim, Y. (2020). '생생인터뷰: 달시 파켓 부산아시아영화학교 교수', *Busan MBC*, 25 May [Online]. Available at: https://busanmbc.co.kr/article/0bw9bWz0q-Y

149      See 'Cup Noodles Museum' website, https://www.cup-noodles-museum.jp/en/osaka_ikeda/about/

150      Jang, J. (2018). '라면의 역사-1963년 국내 첫 라면', *JoongAng Ilbo*, 9 Aug [Online]. Available at: https://news.joins.com/article/22872281

151      Um, D. (2012). 'JYJ "'사생팬', 무단 침입해 키스까지… 일상 무너졌다"', *JoongAng Ilbo*, 9 Mar [Online]. Available at: https://news.joins.com/article/7573153

152      Kim, H. and H. Cho (2012). '월 100만원 쓰는 女사생팬 '알바·노숙 심지어…'', *JoongAng Ilbo*, 15 Mar [Online]. Avaialble

at: https://news.joins.com/article/7621589

153     Joo, J. (2019). '7스킨법이 속건조를 해결해준다고?! 피부과전문의가 공개하는 7스킨법의 진실!', *Dr.Judy* [online]. Available at: https://www.youtube.com/watch?v=xgvvJXkSoy4 [Accessed 25 May 2021].

154     Yoon, A. (2019). 'This Korean Toner Trick Will Give You the Glowing Skin of Your Dreams', *Byrdie*, 9 Jun [online]. Available at: https://www.byrdie.com/7-skin-method

155     Han, J. (2019). '우리 국민이 가장 많이 마시는 술 3 위는 막걸리…1위는', *Maeil Business Newspaper*, 20 Jul [Online]. Available at: https://www.mk.co.kr/news/business/view/2019/07/544416

156     2006 Ministry of Culture, Sports & Tourism Web Archive, https://web.archive.org/web/20141226151623/http://nationalculture.mcst.go.kr/symbol/data/symbol_view.jsp?kcs_seq=58

157     Lee, D. (2019). '쪼그라드는 술 시장서 성장하는 증류식 소주… '화요' '일품진로' '안동소주' 한국판 위스키 약진', *Maeil Business Newspaper*, 9 Jan [Online]. Available at: https://www.mk.co.kr/news/business/view/2019/01/15231/

158     Chosun Ilbo Infographic, http://thestory.chosun.com/site/data/html_dir/2016/08/29/2016082900988.html

159     Cho, I. (2005). 'Moving beyond the green blur: a history of soju', *Korea JoongAng Daily*, 20 Oct [Online]. Available at: https://koreajoongangdaily.joins.com/news/article/article.aspx?aid=2632291

160     Park, M. (2013). '쏘맥 40:127 황금 비율 '애비도 못 알아봐'', *Hankyoreh*, 13 Feb (Online). Available at: https://www.hani.co.kr/arti/specialsection/esc_section/573719.html#csidx-420d36569932e5ab0b0a1206248292b

161     Park, H. (2015). 'Naver to launch global streaming app for K-pop', *The Korea Herald*, 29 Jul [Online]. Available at:http://www.koreaherald.com/view.php?ud=20150729000975

162     Yim, H. (2021). 'FTC gives go ahead for merger deal between V Live and Weverse', *The Korea Herald*, 13 May [Online]. Available at: http://www.koreaherald.com/view.php?ud=20210513000792

163     Song, J., G. Nam, and W.Jang (2014). The Impact of Spread of Webtoon on the Development of Hallyu: The Case Study of Indonesia [웹툰의 확산이 한류의 발전에 미치는 영향 인도네시아 사례를 중심으로]. *Journal of Korea Entertainment Industry Association*, 8(2),  p.359.

164     Park, S. (2009). Actual conditions and problems of Webtoon industry. *Journal of Digital Content & Cultural Policy*, 40, pp.123–158.

165     Harvey, R. C. (1996). *The art of the comic book*. Jackson: University Press of Mississippi, p.162.
See also Kim, J. H., & Yu, J. (2019). Platformizing webtoons: The impact on creative and digital labor in South Korea. *Social Media+ Society*, 5(4), 2056305119880174, pp.2-3.

166     Yun, B. (2013). The differences between the French comics and the Korean Webtoons which are mounted on the digital screen. *Cartoon and Animation Studies*, 32, pp.91–119.

167     Korea Creative Content Agency. (2017). *2017 content industry outlook*. Naju-si, South Korea.
See also Kim, J. H. and Yu, J. (2019), p.3.

168     Choi, J. (2020). 'K-webtoons become mainstream, go global', *The Korea Herald*, 7 May [Online]. Available at: http://www.koreaherald.com/view.php?ud=20200506000728

One of the traditional Korean cultural items that is not covered in this book is "*hanbok*" – traditional Korean clothes. This photo shows girls running through a royal palace in *hanbok*. The sequel to this Glossary will offer a glimpse into the traditional culture of Korea.

A view of central Seoul where traditional and modern Korean cultures are nicely blended.